The IRS and Your Homeschool Organization

Tax Exempt Status for Homeschool Organizations

Carol L Topp, CPA

Ambassador Publishing
Cincinnati, Ohio

Printed in the United States
Second Edition, 2014
ISBN-13: 978-0982924549 ISBN-10: 0982924542
BISAC: Education / Home Schooling
Ambassador Publishing, Cincinnati, Ohio

Book Layout ©2013 BookDesignTemplates.com

Disclaimer and Limitation of Liability
This book is designed to provide accurate and authoritative information about the subject matter covered. The author is not rending legal, accounting, or other professional advice. Any tax advice contained in this book was not intended or written to be used, and cannot be used, by any taxpayer for the purpose of avoiding penalties that may be imposed under the Internal Revenue Code or applicable state or local tax law provisions. Furthermore, this book was not intended or written to support the promotion or marketing of any of the transactions or matters it may address

Please visit www.HomeschoolCPA.com or e-mail the author at Carol@HomeschoolCPA.com

TABLE OF CONTENTS

DEDICATION

Thank you to all the homeschool leaders who have served their members so generously and taught me so much. I admire you immensely.

Carol Topp

Introduction

As the homeschooling movement grows, so do our support groups, co-ops, music and sports programs! This growth means more organization and more structure and needed for homeschool groups.

Perhaps your group has grown and you are wondering if you have any obligation to the IRS. Perhaps your board is asking about being officially recognized as a nonprofit organization. You've heard terms like 'nonprofit,' 'tax-exempt' and '501(c)(3).' Do you understand what they mean?

You may wonder what nonprofit status might mean for your group-good and bad. What are the benefits? What will it cost in dollars and time? Is it needed? Is your group ready?

This book will help you sort out the decisions you need to make. I will discuss the different types of homeschool groups and when they need to worry about taxes and the IRS. I'll explain the pros and cons of being a nonprofit corporation and obtaining 501(c) tax exempt status.

Unlike other books on this subject, I am writing specifically to homeschool organizations. I homeschooled my two daughters, now both grown, for fourteen years. I know how homeschool groups operate and understand their mission. I also know what it is like to be a homeschool leader. You want clear answers and don't have time to read a lot of books or websites. You have no desire to become an expert in nonprofit law—you just want to run a program that benefits homeschooling families.

This second edition includes several recent changes, procedures and forms from the Internal Revenue Service (IRS) that have made obtaining tax exempt status somewhat easier for many small homeschool organizations. But, at the same time, IRS required filings have made life more difficult for many homeschool leaders as well. My goal in this book is to clear the confusion and offer practical assistance. I hope you find it helpful.

Carol Topp, CPA
Cincinnati, Ohio

Chapter One: The IRS and Homeschool Organizations

I'm a homeschool leader and I'm wondering if my group is supposed to be paying taxes to the IRS.

What happens when a homeschool group makes a profit? Do they owe taxes? Is there paperwork with the IRS? Should we hire an accountant?

Homeschool leaders frequently ask questions like the ones above. They are concerned about paying taxes and filing forms, but unlike personal income taxes, homeschool leaders are in unfamiliar territory. They are unsure if their homeschool group is a business or a nonprofit organization and question whether being a nonprofit means they do not owe any taxes. Leaders wonder what their involvement should be with the Internal Revenue Service (IRS).

HOMESCHOOL CONTACT WITH THE IRS

There are several situations when a homeschool organization should be in contact with the IRS:

YOUR HOMESCHOOL GROUP OPENS A CHECKING ACCOUNT AND NEEDS A TAX IDENTIFICATION NUMBER

Usually the first contact a homeschool organization has with the IRS is getting an Employer Identification Number (EIN). Most banks now request an EIN when a group opens a checking account. An EIN is similar to a Social Security Number for a business or nonprofit organization. They are available from the IRS at no charge at www.IRS.gov .

YOUR HOMESCHOOL GROUP PAYS A WORKER

Your worker may be an independent contractor or an employee. Either way, there are forms to file with the IRS at the end of the calendar year (typically a W-2 or a 1099MISC). Additionally, there are employer taxes, such as Social Security or Medicare taxes to pay in addition to worker wages.

YOUR NONPROFIT HOMESCHOOL ORGANIZATION BRINGS IN INCOME OF MORE THAN $5,000 IN A YEAR

If your annual gross revenues are more than $5,000 and you have an educational, religious or charitable purpose, your organization should file for tax exempt status as a 501(c)(3) charitable organization with the IRS. Approval of tax exempt status by the IRS means that your group will not pay income tax on its profit or financial surplus.

YOUR HOMESCHOOL GROUP IS RUN AS A FOR-PROFIT BUSINESS

Most homeschool organizations are operated as nonprofit organizations governed by a board and bylaws, but increasingly some homeschool groups are for-profit businesses. They will need to have a tax number (called an Employer Identification Number or EIN) and file tax returns, such as the Form 1040 Schedule C Business Profit or Loss.

Your group makes money from fund raisers, selling products or selling advertising on your website

Homeschool groups often make money from activities not related to homeschooling. The IRS calls income from these activities "unrelated business income (UBI)" and will tax the profit from these activities. Usually homeschool groups avoid the UBI tax by using one of the IRS exemptions (volunteer labor, selling donated merchandise or unrelated business income of less than $1,000 annually).

The remainder of this book or my other books, especially *Money Management in a Homeschool Organization* and *Paying Workers in a Homeschool Organization*, will discuss these issues in more detail.

Government Intrusion into Homeschoolers' Lives

As a whole, homeschoolers avoid government intrusion in their lives. They have decided to turn down the public education offered to them by their local government and educate their children on their own, so naturally, many homeschool leaders are resistant to local, state or federal governments interfering with their right to homeschool. This resistance continues when they wish to band together in homeschool co-ops or support groups and find themselves facing taxes, IRS rules and employment regulations.

In general, a homeschool leader usually deals with a government agency on behalf of his or her group and not as an individual homeschool parent. In this book, I will be addressing the group's interaction with the IRS and state governments, not an individual's dealing with the government.

As a homeschool leader wishing to do things legally and correctly, you may feel as though the government agencies are "harassing" you.

Sometimes the regulations seem overly complex for a small organization. That is frequently true, but do not misinterpret these rules and regulations as restricting your freedom to homeschool. There are usually established to keep unscrupulous people from committing fraud or self-dealing under the guise of a nonprofit organization. We all live with excess regulations put into place because someone going before us has been dishonest. Homeschool leaders are no different; they must play by the rules of the game or they will be suspect of being dishonest also.

HISTORICAL PERSPECTIVE ON CHARITIES AND TAXES

Many homeschool leaders view the IRS like most taxpayers: as the big bad wolf coming to blow down their house and leave them penniless. But to a homeschool leader the IRS can be a friend and ally, and not the enemy.

Since the early days of the Puritans and Quakers in America, the United States has had a history of charitable organizations doing what governments cannot or should not do including founding hospitals, orphanages, schools, churches and libraries. Many charities were founded on the religious principles of helping others. Some early Americans feared that if the government provided charitable services, it would give rise to a rebirth of the monarchy. So they promoted private charities via the tax code. The Revenue Act of 1913 established the income tax system with tax exemption for certain organizations. It contained language allowing tax exemption for "charitable, religious and educational purposes" taken from legislation dating back to 1894. In 1927 tax deductions for charitable donations were allowed. [1]

The US tax code allows most nonprofit organizations to apply for and be granted tax-exempt (i.e. tax free) status. That means that no income taxes are paid on your profits and therefore can stay with your group to be used in the future. For-profit businesses do not have this advantage. They pay income taxes of 15-35% (or more) of their profit. Additionally, most states follow the federal tax exemption and do not tax nonprofits on their surplus income. Some even grant sales and property tax exemption to nonprofits in their state.

This tax exempt status is something for which to be grateful and to participate in fully if your group is eligible. There is paperwork and a one-time IRS filing fee, but once tax exempt status is granted, it is a right and privilege to be appreciated, not avoided.

Several times I have had leaders tell me that they don't want to get involved with the IRS. So, I explain that unfortunately that might not be possible. Instead, I explain that the IRS tax exempt status should be seen as an advantage to their organization and not something to be avoided. It is not every society in the world that is so generous to its charitable and nonprofit organizations. For instance, in Austria, charities are mainly subject to tax, but are exempted from paying income tax if the given purpose of the charity is related to public welfare. Homeschool groups may not be tax exempt in Austria.[2] If Americans do not exercise their rights, we are in danger of losing them.

Does Tax Exempt Status Limit Homeschool Freedoms?

Via my website, HomeschoolCPA.com, I am frequently asked questions such as this one from a homeschool leader:

> Some of the people in our group that have had some experiences with 501(c)(3) status said that the government has made them open their group up to individuals that they would not normally allow in their group because they are a government entity (like permitting someone not in our faith to teach a class).

This leader has been misled. Receiving 501(c)(3) tax exempt status from the IRS does not make a homeschool organization a government entity; it simply means that the group is exempt from paying income tax on their profit and that donors can make tax-deductible contributions. It is a tax status.

Additionally, having tax exempt status does not mean that a group must open up their membership. Some nonprofits as private organizations are not subject to the anti-discrimination laws which might apply to for-profit organizations. For example, the Boy Scouts of America do not allow girls as Cub Scouts or Boy Scouts, and the courts have held this does not violate anti-discrimination laws.

Americans still have religious freedom and freedom to assemble. While there are anti-discrimination rules in the United States, we still have the right to "discriminate" on the basis of religion. Homeschool organizations are free to choose their members and teachers or exclude members in order to maintain a common religious belief. Does a Catholic school have to allow non-Catholics teach their classes? Of course not.

The Boy Scouts won a very important Supreme Court case in 2000 allowing them to exclude homosexual men from being Boy Scout leaders. The Supreme Court determined that the Boy Scouts had the freedom of association, which allows a private organization to exclude a person from membership when "the presence of that person affects in a significant way the group's ability to advocate public or private viewpoints."[3]

In summary, do not fear the IRS, but instead be thankful we Americans can exercise our rights and freedoms to homeschool and to assemble together in a support group, homeschool co-op, music or sports programs. In addition, many homeschool organizations may be exempted from paying income tax on their profits. The remainder of this book will discuss tax exemption for these organizations.

[2]

Chapter Two: What Does Tax Exempt Status Mean?

Nonprofit Status is Not the Same as Tax Exempt

Many homeschool leaders are confused by the words "non profit" and "tax exempt." They are not the same thing. Nonprofit is a status conferred by state law for organizations that are organized and operate as nonprofits. Tax exempt status is conferred by the Internal Revenue Service to qualified nonprofit organizations granting them freedom from federal income tax.

Think of it like being in love and getting married. Being a nonprofit is like being in love. You have passion and act like it. But it's not until you are married that you gain tax benefits from the IRS. Similarly, your nonprofit will not have tax advantages until it applies for tax exempt status with the IRS. (Fortunately, the IRS offers several exemptions to submitting paperwork for tax exempt status. More on that later.).

Naturally, like many couples in love who get married, the vast majority of nonprofit organizations pursue tax exempt status. After all, they eligible for tax exemption and can use their financial surplus to fund their mission and activities rather than pay taxes.

OPERATE AND ORGANIZE LIKE A NONPROFIT

Your organization is a nonprofit organization if you do two things: operate like a nonprofit and organize like one. To operate like a nonprofit means that you have a mission other than making a profit. For homeschool groups their mission is usually social (like support groups) or educational (like co-ops, music groups or youth sports teams).

To be organized like a nonprofit usually means you have a board, not a single owner, and have some type of organizing document such as bylaws, Articles of Association (for unincorporated associations) or Articles of Incorporation (for nonprofit corporations). These documents usually spell out your mission, membership requirements and board duties.

Many people incorrectly think that there is some paperwork to "register" with their state to be a nonprofit organization, but this is not usually the case. Paperwork is not filed with your state until (and if) you decide to become a nonprofit corporation or if you do fundraising and solicit donations from the public. Many states (usually the Attorney General's office) then require you to register and explain your fundraising activities.

Sometimes homeschool leaders will tell me their homeschool group is *not* a nonprofit, meaning they have never filed any paperwork with their state or the IRS. I explain if they are not a nonprofit, then they are a for profit business! "No; we're not that either! We're run by a board, not an owner," they explain. So I advise them to call themselves what they are: an unincorporated nonprofit association.

DEFINITION OF TAX EXEMPT

Tax exempt status is recognized by the IRS to qualified organizations. There are over 20 types of tax exempt status including charities, schools, hospitals, veterans organizations, trade and business leagues, hobby clubs, and even cemeteries! The most popular by far is the tax exempt status called "qualified charity" explained in Section 501(c)(3) of the IRS Code. Approximately 80% of all tax exempt organizations are 501(c)(3) "qualified charities."

Tax exempt status for 501(c)(3) organizations is not automatically granted just because your organization is a nonprofit; it must (usually) be applied for with the IRS. There are a few specific instances where 501(c)(3) tax exempt status is granted without formally applying:

1. Churches and auxiliaries of churches.

2. Organizations with annual gross revenues less than $5,000 per year.

These very small charities are granted all the benefits of 501(c)(3) status without filing the official paperwork with the IRS, but they still are required to file an annual information return with the IRS (Form 990, 900EZ or 990-N). Churches are not required to file an annual information return with the IRS.

So what is 501(c)(3) status and can your homeschool group qualify? From the Internal Revenue Service comes this definition of a 501(c)(3) organization:

> (3) Corporations, and any community chest, fund, or foundation, organized and operated exclusively for religious, charitable, scientific, testing for public safety, literary, or educational purposes, or to foster national or international amateur sports competition (but only if no part of its activities involve the provision of athletic facilities or equipment), or for the prevention of cruelty to children or animals, no part of the net earnings of which inures to the benefit of any private shareholder or individual, no substantial part of the activities of

which is carrying on propaganda, or otherwise attempting, to influence legislation (except as otherwise provided in subsection (h)), and which does not participate in, or intervene in (including the publishing or distributing of statements), any political campaign on behalf of (or in opposition to) any candidate for public office.[4][5]

If that is too full of "legalese" for you, try this definition from Wikipedia, the free on-line encyclopedia:

501(c)(3) is a section of the US tax code that defines a type of nonprofit organization that is dominant in the United States. The term refers to:

* Section 501. Exemption from tax on corporations, certain trusts, etc.

* Subsection (c) List of exempt organizations

* Sub-subsection (3) Corporations, and any community chest, fund, or foundation, organized and operated exclusively for religious, charitable, scientific, testing for public safety, literary, or educational purposes, or to foster national or international amateur sports competition, or for the prevention of cruelty to children or animals.

Section 501(c)(3) is just one of the sections in the Internal Revenue Code which grants tax exemption to nonprofit organizations, but it is also the most common one. For this reason, nonprofit organizations in general are often referred to as "501(c)(3) organizations" or similar.

501(c)(3) status is important to many charitable groups. Not only does the group avoid paying taxes on income, but the donor may deduct their donations from their income for tax purposes. Some individuals and groups (and virtually all foundations) will not give to a charity if it does not have 501(c)(3) status. Therefore, loss of this status can be harmful to a charity's existence.[6]

This is a pretty good definition. As you can see, there are many types of organizations that can be called 501(c)(3) from a church to the Humane Society.

Many homeschool organizations, especially co-ops, are formed for educational purposes and are qualified for 501(c)(3) status.

WE'RE NOT 501(C)(3) AND DON'T WANT TO BE!

I was a little surprised when a homeschool leader emailed me to say,

> "We not a 501(c)(3) and don't want to be! It would take so much work, money, etc. to be a 501(c)(3)! Our group does not take donations. Membership fees cover our cost of doing business."

I think she failed to see 501(c)(3) status for its benefits. She saw only the paperwork and, as we all know, paying taxes costs money and involves paperwork too! She probably incorrectly assumed that her nonprofit organization didn't owe any tax. I explained that if her organization made a profit, it owes tax on that profit unless it is legally tax exempt. Just because her homeschool group does not accept donations does not exempt them from the IRS and tax filing regulations.

Another homeschool support group leader told me that they "never filed anything with the IRS because all the money we bring in goes right back out every year." This group was certainly operating like a nonprofit with no profits, but being financially insolvent does not automatically make your organization tax exempt either.

Both these leaders had the right motive, but incorrectly assumed there organizations were free from paying taxes or applying for tax exempt status. The USA offers a wonderful opportunity for nonprofit groups to keep all of their surplus and avoid paying taxes on it, but it does mean filing a document (Form 1023 or 1024) with the IRS to become a tax exempt organization.

Homeschool Support Groups

While homeschool co-ops may be eligible to be tax exempt as 501(c)(3) educational organizations, many homeschool groups are formed for support of the homeschooling family. Indeed, in the beginning of the homeschool movement these support groups were the only type of homeschool group. There were not enough homeschooled children to form a co-op or a sports league, but parents still gathered for support.

Homeschool support groups may qualify as tax exempt under a different section of the IRS code, 501(c)(7) for social and recreational clubs. According to IRS guidelines, a social club exists for pleasure or recreation and includes personal contact and fellowship. These criteria might fit a homeschool support group. The members of most homeschool support groups are limited to homeschool parents, they meet for social reasons, and are supported by membership fees (and maybe a little bit of fund raisers), but do not sell products or services and do not collect tax deductible donations.

Most homeschool support groups can be considered 501(c)(7) Social Clubs.

Here are the criteria to be classified as a 501(c)(7) Social Club.

1. Purpose: pleasure, social or recreation. A nonprofit motive and no part of the net earnings may inure to the benefit of any person having a personal and private interest in the activities of the organization. There must be an established membership of individuals, personal contacts and fellowship. A commingling of the members must play a major role in the life of the organization. Common examples include college fraternities or sororities, country clubs, garden clubs, hobby clubs, etc.

2. Limited membership: Membership is limited and consistent with the character of the club.

3. Supported by membership fees. In general, a social club should be supported solely by membership fees, dues, and assessments. A 501(c)(7) organization can receive up to 35% of its gross receipts from sources outside of its membership without losing its tax exempt status. For example, up to 35% of your total revenues can come from fund raising.

4. Business activities. If your club will engage in business, such as selling products or services, it generally will be denied tax exempt status. However, your organization can provide meals, refreshments, or services related to its exempt purposes only to its own members or their dependents or guests.

5. Tax treatment of donations. Donations to social and recreation clubs are not deductible as charitable contributions on the donor's federal income tax return.

Most homeschool co-ops do not fit this description of a social club because they sell services (classes) and have an educational purpose, not a social or recreational purpose. They may qualify for 501(c)(3) tax exempt status as an educational organization.

COMPARISON OF 501(C)(3) QUALIFIED CHARITY AND 501(C)(7) SOCIAL CLUB

For homeschool leaders the difference in 501(c)(3) qualified charity status and 501(c)(7) social club boils down to the organization's purpose. A nonprofit organization must have an educational purpose (or religious, charitable, scientific, literary purpose, or to foster national or international amateur sports competition) to qualify for 501(c)(3) status.

But there are other major differences as well. 501(c)(3) organizations may accept tax deductible donations, but donations to 501(c)(7) social clubs are not tax deductible to the donor.

Additionally, social clubs do not have to file an application with the IRS to receive tax exempt status. Social clubs may "self-proclaim" their tax exempt status. Here is how the IRS explains the requirement to file for tax exempt status:

> It is true the Tax Reform Act of 1969 requirement to "give notice," (to apply for recognition of tax-exempt status) applies only to organizations wanting section 501(c)(3) status.
>
> So, although other types of organizations are not required to file Form 1024, they may still wish to do so in order to receive a determination letter of IRS recognition of their status. Having the determination letter ensures public recognition of their status and may enable exemption from some state taxes.
>
> Also, even though an organization may "self-proclaim" its tax-exempt status, it is still subject to the rules governing its particular subsection. It is also subject to IRS examination to determine whether it meets the requirements for the exemption it is claiming. [7]

As the IRS stated above, a 501(c)(7) social club does not have to file the Form 1024 to be tax exempt. Most homeschool support groups forgo filing the form and save pay the IRS filing fee of $400 too. But the IRS still requires all nonprofit organizations to file an information return, the Form 990, 990-EZ or 990-N every year. See Chapter Ten for details.

If your organization wishes to obtain 501(c)(3) tax exempt status, then you must file an application, IRS Form 1023, and pay the associated fee. Alternatively, if you fit the criteria of a social club, then your organization can "self-proclaim" that you are tax exempt without filing the paperwork.

You may be confused about whether your homeschool organization is a 501(c)(3) "qualified charity" or 501(c)(7) social club. This chart[8] explains the difference:

Comparison of 501(c)(3) Qualified Charity and 501(c)(7) Social Club

	501(c)(3) Qualified Charity	501(c)(7) Social Club
Purpose	Religious, Educational, Charitable, Scientific, Literary	Pleasure, recreation, social activities
Examples	churches, charities, private schools, **homeschool co-ops with an educational purpose**	Fraternities, sororities, country clubs, hobby clubs, **homeschool support groups**
Requirements	No private inurement allowed. Upon dissolution all assets must be distributed to another 501(c)(3) organization.	Personal contact, fellowship and co-mingling of members. No private inurement allowed.
Activities	Can hold programs, sell services and products as part of their exempt purpose.	Can provide meals or services only to members in connection with club activities
Tax deductible donations allowed	Yes	No
Tax exempt (no taxes on profits)	Exempt from Federal income tax unless the organization has unrelated business income	Exempt from Federal income tax on income derived from members; other income taxed
Source of Income	Membership fees, fees for services, donations, fund raisers, program fees	Primarily (65% or more) from membership fees.
Membership	Open to public	Limited membership and consistent with the purpose of the club.
IRS Application Required?	Yes, if gross revenues over $5,000/year. File Form 1023	No. The IRS does not require 501(c)(7) organizations to file an application. They can "self-proclaim" tax exempt status.
Annual IRS Reporting	Form 990N, Form 99EZ or Form 990	Form 990N, Form 99EZ or Form 990
Legislative Lobbying permitted?	Insubstantial lobbying allowed (less than 20% of total expenses). No endorsement of a candidate.	No limit on legislative activity as long as it furthers the exempt purpose

WHAT IF WE ARE NOT A CHARITY?

Do not be confused by the IRS's use of the word "charity." To them it means more than helping the poor. It means promoting the common good through education, the arts, civil rights, public works and other meaningful endeavors. Your group does not have to operate as a charity, meaning free tuition or free books unless it desires to do so. Most homeschool co-ops may offer low fees, but do not usually offer free classes. They have an educational purpose, not a pure charitable focus. Some homeschool groups might have a charitable emphasis and several have established special funds to help financially strapped families, but their main purpose is still education, not charity.

CAN MY HOMESCHOOL BE TAX EXEMPT?

In this book, I am addressing tax exemption for homeschool organizations and groups such as support groups, co-ops, clubs, music programs and sports teams. But what about an individual family? I am frequently asked if a person or a homeschooling family can receive tax exempt status, such as these two parents asked:

> I am interested in writing proposals for grants for my family's home school. As an individual home school, not as a home school support group, I want to apply to receive small amounts of money for travel, museum entry, art gallery entry, books, posters, etc. What do I have to do to have our home school be exempt from federal taxation?

> I wonder if I could set my own family's homeschool up as a nonprofit. In my state, homeschools are considered a private school.

Homeschool organizations operating as nonprofit tax exempt organizations have many benefits including tax free income, discounts, and sometimes pay no sales tax. Many fund raising organizations and grants now require 501(c)(3) tax exempt status to participate. It is only natural for homeschoolers to think these benefits should apply to them as individuals, since they apply to many homeschool groups.

A private individual or family cannot be a tax exempt organization. The reason is that the IRS does not allow tax exempt organizations to offer private benefits or what they call "inurement" (meaning to become beneficial or advantageous) to individuals.

A nonprofit organization exists to serve a group, not an individual. The IRS will not grant "recognized charity" tax exempt status to a group that is formed solely to benefit the founder's family. A tax exempt organization must serve a public good. The IRS forbids inurement in tax exempt organizations. Inurement occurs when an organization allows the individuals in control to profit from the organization. Organizations can lose their tax exempt status for practicing inurement.

From the IRS website comes this explanation:

Inurement/Private Benefit – Charitable Organizations

A section 501(c)(3) organization must not be organized or operated for the benefit of private interests, such as the creator or the creator's family, shareholders of the organization, other designated individuals, or persons controlled directly or indirectly by such private interests. No part of the net earnings of a section 501(c)(3) organization may inure to the benefit of any private shareholder or individual. A private shareholder or individual is a person having a personal and private interest in the activities of the organization. [9]

A individual homeschool is not eligible for the benefits of 501(c)(3) tax exempt status, even if a state classifies a homeschool as a private school.

SUMMARY

501(c)(3) status tax exempt status is available for organizations that have a specific purpose that is religious, charitable, scientific, testing for public safety, literary, educational, to foster national or international amateur sports competition, or for the prevention of cruelty to children or animals. Most homeschool co-ops, sports or music programs that have an educational purpose could qualify for 501(c)(3) tax exempt status.

Homeschool support groups with a social purpose may qualify for tax exempt status as a 501(c)(7) social club. Individual homeschool families cannot receive tax exempt status.

Most of this book will focus on 501(c)(3) tax exempt status for homeschool organizations with an educational purpose. The 501(c)(3) status is more common and has more IRS regulations. The next chapter will discuss the benefits and costs of applying for 501(c)(3) tax exempt status.

[3]

Chapter Three: Benefits and Costs of 501(c)(3) Tax Exempt Status

A nonprofit organization can exist in several forms from a simple unincorporated, informal organization to a large, structured tax exempt organization. To help your sort out the various terms, I have created a diagram to explain the common nonprofit forms.

COMMON NON PROFIT FORMS

A pyramid can visually explain the common forms a nonprofit homeschool organization can take. The bottom of the pyramid is the least organized type of homeschool group. They are usually small groups, without a formal board or bylaws. They may not even have a checking account in the organization's name because they deal in small amounts of cash.

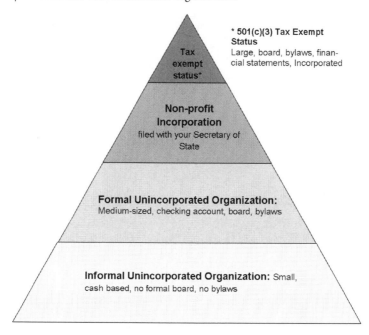

As an organization grows, it may climb up the pyramid, to become a more formal unincorporated organizations. The organization increases in structure by adopting bylaws, forming a board, and opening a checking account.

It is typical for homeschool groups to start at the unincorporated level (at the base of the pyramid). They can exist at that level for as long as they wish and only progress to another level as their program and membership demands increase. It is more common for homeschool co-ops to seek nonprofit incorporation and tax exempt status (the top two levels of the pyramid). Support groups typically remain unincorporated organizations.

As discussed in Chapter Two, a homeschool group can have a social or educational purpose. Some homeschool groups start as support groups (and are recognized by the IRS as 501(c)(7) social clubs), and may add classes or co-ops. Their structures and finances increase as they add these educational programs. Their purpose shifts from purely social to more educational. At some point, they need to consider non-profit incorporation in their state and applying for 501(c)(3) status with the IRS.

BENEFITS OF 501(C)(3) STATUS

There are several benefits of 501(c)(3) status tax exempt status. By far the most valuable benefit is the exemption from paying tax on your group's financial surplus. Additionally, many organizations consider the ability to provide a tax deduction to donors for their contributions as a significant benefit. Other benefits include discounts, prestige and participation in special programs.

TAX EXEMPTION

The IRS allows organizations that have applied for and received tax exempt status to avoid paying income tax on their profit or surplus. This is a tremendous benefit because it allows the organization to re-invest their surplus into their mission rather than paying income tax. Many states also allow exemption from state income tax as well as other taxes such as property, sales and franchise taxes.

Word of caution: IRS tax exemption applies to federal income tax. It does not apply to employer taxes (Social Security and Medicare taxes). If you hire and pay employees, your organization must still file and pay payroll taxes. See my ebook *Paying Workers in a Homeschool Organization* for details on paying workers. It is available at HomeschoolCPA.com.

CONTRIBUTIONS

A significant benefit of 501(c)(3) status is not for the charity, but for its donors. Contributions of cash or property to a qualified charity are tax deductible. This is an important benefit and many organizations pursue the paperwork of 501(c)(3) status simply to receive more donations. If your homeschool group is not receiving donations (i.e., if you are funded by solely by member fees), you may not consider this as a significant advantage, but if you have individuals or businesses that wish to make donations, but will not unless they are tax deductible, you will need the IRS's coveted 501(c)(3) "qualified charity" status.

If you are seeking government or charitable foundation grants, you will need 501(c)(3) status. Competition for grants is stiff and grants are rarely awarded to organization without 501(c)(3) status.

DISCOUNTS

There are other benefits of 501(c)(3) status including special discounts on postage and discounts on rent, insurance or equipment offered by some businesses. Some states offer special status to nonprofits such as sales tax exemptions on purchases made by the nonprofit or property tax exemptions. Check with your state's Department of Revenue to see if 501(c)(3) status is required for these benefits. Sometimes it is not required.

PRESTIGE

One intangible benefit of the 501(c)(3) status is prestige. When I see a nonprofit organization state that they are a 501(c)(3) nonprofit organization, I know that they are serious in their mission, they expect to be around awhile and they went to extra effort to be accountable. It gives me assurance that they are trying to run a responsible organization.

SPECIAL PROGRAMS

Some special programs, especially fund raising programs are only open to 501(c)(3) organizations. Our local grocery "Rewards Program" requires that a group be a 501(c)(3) tax exempt organization to participate. Just being a nonprofit corporation registered by the state as a charitable organization is not enough and non-501(c)(3) organizations cannot participate. One homeschool co-op in my area applied for 501(c)(3) status specifically to participate in a fund raiser. Box Tops for Education now requires homeschool organizations to have 501(c)(3) status to participate in their popular fund raiser.

Some communities have a discounted office supply store only open to 501(c)(3) organizations. These stores offer furniture and paper, but they only sell to 501(c)(3) organizations. Often large companies give away software and computers, but only to 501(c)(3) organizations.

DISADVANTAGES OF 501(C)(3) STATUS

The disadvantages of 501(c)(3) tax exempt status include fees, paperwork, government imposed limitations and annual reporting to the IRS and your state.

COST

The costs to apply for 501(c)(3) tax exempt status can add up. The application fee to the IRS is $400 for organizations with gross annual revenues under $10,000. The fee increases to $850 for organizations with gross annual revenues over $10,000. These fees and thresholds are subject to change.

In July 2014, the IRS introduced a new, shorter application for 501(c)(3) status, the Form 1023-EZ. Only small organizations with annual gross revenues of less than $50,000 are eligible to use the Form 1023-EZ. The fee to file the form is $400. Learn more about the Form 1023-EZ in Chapter Nine.

In addition to the IRS filing fee, are the fees for state incorporation which can vary widely. My home state of Ohio charges $150 for nonprofit incorporation, while our neighboring state, Indiana charges

$30. Visit http://www.hurwitassociates.com for a listing of incorporation fees for your state.

Many organizations hire professional assistance from either a lawyer or an accountant to help them with the IRS application (Form 1023). Fees can range from $500 to $1500 and up. I offer services for preparing Form 1023 or reviewing a self-prepared application. Visit http://HomeschoolCPA.com and click on the Products page for my current fees and services.

PAPERWORK

The paperwork to apply for 501(c)(3) status can be daunting. The IRS has two forms, the longer Form 0123 or the shorter 1023-EZ. Organizations with annual gross revenues of $50,000 or less and assets of $250,000 or less may be eligible to file the shorter, Form 1023-EZ. The IRS has other qualifications that you can read about in the Eligibility Checklist found in the instructions to the Form 1023-EZ at http://IRS.gov .

The application form for the IRS (Form 1023) is 28 pages long! The instructions for Form 1023 are another 38 pages long! Form 1023 asks for these documents:

- Bylaws
- Articles of Incorporation or "organizing documents"
- Policy manuals
- Mission or purpose statements
- Explanation of activities
- History of your organization
- List of board members names and addresses
- Five years of financial statements
- List of donors and amounts donated

The Form 1023-EZ does not request any of this information. It does require an organization to attest that they have proper organizing documents, but does not request to see them. Some organizations may find they need to spend time assembling the paperwork before they can begin the 501(c)(3) application process.

LIMITATIONS

One of the greatest detriments to 501(c)(3) tax exempt status are the limitations the IRS imposes. Particularly limiting is the political involvement of 501(c)(3) organizations. The IRS does not allow for 501(c)(3) organizations to collect tax deductible donations that could then be funneled to a political candidate. For that reason, 501(c)(3) organizations are limited in their political activities. A 501(c)(3) organization can lobby for legislation, but cannot endorse a candidate for local, state or federal office. Nonpartisan educational activities are allowed. For homeschool groups this means you may write emails to inform your memberships about bills and referendums (i.e. legislation) that may impact their homeschooling or parental rights. You may not endorse or promote a candidate for office. Specifically not permitted are:

- Statements in support or in opposition to a candidate either verbally or in writing
- Candidate rating
- Receiving donations for a candidate
- Preferential treatment to a candidate (i.e., if you invite a candidate to address your homeschool group, you must give equal opportunity for the opponents to address your group)

Many groups find these limitations quite easy to live with because they are mainly active in educational lobbying and not political candidate endorsement. But, occasionally, a candidate runs for office that is so homeschool-friendly that a group wants to support him or her. In my town, we had a former homeschool mother run for school board. A homeschool group invited her to a meeting and prayed for her strength and wisdom. Was that in violation of the IRS rules? No, because the homeschool support group was not a 501(c)(3) organization, and therefore was free to promote this candidate. Some groups find that they are uninterested in 501(c)(3) status because they wish to endorse candidates and be active politically. One solution to these groups is to split off their political activities into a separate group.

ANNUAL REPORTING

Another disadvantage of 501(c)(3) status is the annual reporting. Your contact with the IRS is not over when you get your letter of 501(c)(3) status (called a determination letter). All 501(c)(3) organizations (except churches) must file an annual information return called Form 990 (or 990-EZ or 990-N) with the IRS. This is not a tax return, because tax exempt organizations are not generally required to pay income tax[10], but it certainly looks like a tax return! The IRS asks detailed questions about activities, finances, fund raising, donations and board members.

Organizations with annual gross revenues under $50,000 can file the much shorter Form 990-N. The Form 990-N has only seven questions and is filed online. There is no paper version. The Form 990-N asks a few fairly simple questions such as name, Employer Identification Number (EIN), a contact person's name, address and if your organization had gross revenues under $50,000. Learn more about the Form 990, 990-EZ and 990-N in Chapter Ten.

If you do need to file a Form 990, I recommend you hire an accountant to assist you. The Form 990 is more complicated than many corporate tax returns. Find a professional that is knowledgeable about nonprofit accounting. Many accountants focus on businesses and personal taxes, but not the specific laws for nonprofits. Through my accounting practice, I offer Form 990 return preparation. I also will review a 990 return you prepare. Visit my website http://HomeschoolCPA.com for current services and prices.

Your state may also have reporting requirements, although many states accept the IRS Form 990. This avoids duplication of effort. Visit http://www.hurwitassociates.com/ for a listing of reporting requirement for your state.

Do not let this list of disadvantages discourage you from pursuing 501(c)(3) status. I do not mean to scare you off, but to help you to know the obstacles in the path. Most groups find these limitations or disadvantages easy to live with and decide the advantages far outweigh the disadvantages. See also Chapter Ten "We're Tax Exempt! Now What?" for more information.

[4]

Chapter Four: Alternatives to 501(c)(3)Tax Exempt Status

> Does my homeschool support group really need to apply to 501(c)(3) tax exempt status with the IRS? It seems like a lot of time and money. We have a small budget and we don't accept tax deductible donations. Can't we just operate as we are?

Many homeschool leaders can identify with the leader's situation above. This chapter will discuss the alternatives to applying for 501(c)(3) tax exempt status.

Many larger homeschool organizations, especially co-ops that have an educational purpose, seek 501(c)(3) tax exempt status for its many benefits:

- tax exemption from federal income tax
- ability to accept tax deductible donations
- ability to participate in fund raisers only open to 501(c)(3) charities

Seeking tax exempt status has many benefits, the foremost being tax exemption, but 501(c)(3) tax exempt status is not automatically granted. An organization must specifically request 501(c)(3) tax exempt from the Internal Revenue Service (IRS).

FILE EARLY

Many small nonprofit organizations mistakenly believe that they must apply for 501(c)(3) status when the reach a specific dollar amount, but that is not necessarily the case. Your organization should request tax exempt status when it has a financial surplus and wishes to avoid paying taxes on that surplus or wish to receive tax deductible donations. Sometimes there are advantages to applying while your organization is still small and new, such as reduced filing fees to the IRS.

Failure to request tax exempt status, means your organization could be liable for income tax on any surplus you have at the end of the year.

The IRS expects nonprofit organizations to apply to 501(c)(3) status within 15 months of their formation. Legal formation is usually dated from the date an organization files for nonprofit incorporation in their state. If an organization never incorporates, the date of formation may be when they began activities or applied for an Employer Identification Number (EIN) with the IRS. The IRS does allow an automatic extension of 12 months, making the deadline for application a total of 27 months after formation.

If an organization files for tax exempt status after the 27 month period, the IRS will date their exemption from the date of the application (i.e. the date the IRS received the Form 1023 applying for 501(c)(3) status). They will not back date tax exempt status to the date of formation without an explanation of why the organization was delayed in applying.

A nonprofit organization could be liable for income tax on any profits earned in the years before tax exemption was requested. For that reason, nonprofits should apply for tax exempt status within 27 months of formation, preferably earlier.

Small Nonprofits

The IRS allows very small nonprofit organizations the benefits of 501(c)(3) tax exemption without filing the Form 1023 if their annual gross revenue is normally not more than $5,000. (See Instructions for Form 1023, page 1 at http://www.irs.gov/pub/irs-pdf/i1023.pdf).

A leader of a small homeschool organization desired written proof of their tax exempt status for banking purposes, but had no desire to go through the 501(c)(3) application process. Her organization's annual gross revenues were under $5,000, so she was not required to file the Form 1023 or 1023-EZ. Instead, I contacted the IRS on her behalf and they were mailed a letter stating the following:

> "We have no record that your organization has been recognized as exempt from federal income tax. ...an organization organized and operated exclusively for 501(c)(3) purposes...does not have to file for exemption unless its annual gross receipts are normally more than $5,000."

If you are a small homeschool nonprofit (gross revenues under $5,000 a year), and desire a letter from the IRS explaining that you are tax exempt, do what I did and call the IRS. The phone number for Exempt Organizations is 1-877-829-5500. Request a letter explaining the exemption for filing a Form 1023 for very small nonprofits.

If your homeschool organization brings in more than $5,000 a year, it is time to apply for tax exempt status with the IRS (or time to start paying tax on your surplus!). $5,000 is a pretty small amount of money; even a very small organization can have gross revenues of $5,000 a year. Note that the measure is gross revenue, meaning all your revenue, not just your profit.

So what should you do when your organization starts bringing in more than $5,000 a year?

Larger Nonprofits

If your organization has gross revenue of more than $5,000 annually, there are several options:

- File form 1023 or 1023-EZ, if eligible, with the IRS and become a 501(c)(3) tax exempt "qualified charity."
- Determine if another type of tax exempt status with the IRS, such as 501(c)(7) a social club better describes your organization.
- Ask a church or another 501(c)(3) organization to take you under their tax exempt umbrella as a ministry or in a fiscal sponsorship arrangement.
- Reorganize your organization to stay small (i.e. keep your gross income under $5,000 per year).
- Pay income taxes.

These options are ranked in rough order of preference for ease in obtaining each and the advantages to the organization.

File for 501(c)(3) Qualified Charity Status

There are certainly advantages to becoming a 501(c)(3) tax exempt organization, but they come at a cost. Read about the pros and cons of 501(c)(3) status in Chapter Three. The application process for 501(c)(3) tax exempt status can be a big undertaking, but the benefits are substantial. Most organizations seek professional help in applying, since it is an undertaking they will only pursue once in their organization's lifetime.

Your organization does not need an attorney to apply for 501(c)(3) status, but it may be helpful to talk to a lawyer if you are constructing a complicated organizational structure such as one nonprofit corporation controlling another (for example, a nonprofit and its foundation), or a for-profit and nonprofit being closely controlled by a common group.

The IRS application for 501(c)(3) status is a 28-page application (IRS Form 1023) and involves a good amount of financial reporting. You will need to supply five years of financial history or two years of projected budgets if your organization is brand new. A knowledgeable CPA can be helpful in preparing these statements. Smaller organizations (annual gross revenues under $50,000) may be eligible to file the shorter Form 1023-EZ. See Chapter Nine "The Application Process" for some helpful tips. This is the option most pursued by homeschool co-ops.

Determine Eligibility for an Alternative Tax Exempt Status with the IRS

Some nonprofit organizations may qualify to be a 501(c)(4) social welfare organization or 501(c)(7) social club tax exempt organization instead of a 501(c)(3) qualified charity. A 501(c)(4) is a social welfare organization that exists to promote the common good and general welfare of the people in a community. Examples include unions, trade organizations, the American Association of Retired Persons (AARP) and the National Association for the Advancement of Colored People (NAACP). A 501(c)(7) is a social club with limited membership whose main purpose is to gather face-to-face for fellowship and pleasure. Examples include college fraternities or sororities, country clubs and private pool and tennis clubs. Homeschool support groups may fit under the 501(c)(7) definition of a social club. See Chapter Two for a full explanation of 501(c)(7) social club status.

Social welfare organizations and social clubs are tax-exempt like 501(c)(3) organizations, but donations are not tax deductible. This could be a major drawback if your organization is planning or hoping to receive donations. Also, some fund raising programs may be limited to 501(c)(3) qualified charities, so 501(c)(4) social welfare organizations or 501(c)(7) social clubs would not be allowed to participate.

501(c)(4)s are allowed greater freedom in political lobbying and endorsements than 501(c)(3) organizations. For example, the Ohio Society of CPAs, a 501(c)(4) trade organization, endorses candidates for state auditor and treasurer.

Homeschool organizations should carefully research the difference between 501(c)(3) qualified charity and 501(c)(4) social welfare and 501(c)(7) social club status. Consult an experienced CPA or nonprofit attorney before making your decision. I am available to assist homeschool groups in making the decision by private phone consultation. Feel free to reach me by email at HomeschoolCPA.com if you wish to schedule a phone consultation.

Read more about 501(c) organizations at the IRS webpage at http://www.irs.gov/charities/nonprofits/index.html and click Requirements for Exemption.

MINISTRY OF A CHURCH OR FISCAL SPONSORSHIP

There are many advantages to having a church willing to take your homeschool group in as one of its ministries. You can usually benefit from the church's tax exempt status, facility, leadership, and bank account! Churches are automatically tax exempt and do not need to apply for 501(c)(3) status with the IRS nor do they have to file an annual information returns with the IRS (the Form 990/990-EZ/990-N). If your homeschool group is one of the church's ministries, you do not have to have any dealings with the IRS (unless you pay workers).

Fiscal sponsorship is a formal arrangement where an established tax exempt nonprofit organization acts as an umbrella for a project or group that does not have its own tax-exempt status. It is a method to get a new organization launched quickly and allow it immediate advantages of tax exempt status. The umbrella organization lets the new organization use their tax exempt status to raise funds and launch their programs.

The arrangement is usually temporary, just a year or two until the new organization is spun off to be independent. It is common for the sponsoring organization to charge a fee (1-5% of the revenues) for overseeing and advising the new group.

Your organization may find an established homeschool group with 501(c)(3) status willing to take you under their umbrella for a few years. They may provide advice, use of their Employer Identification Number (EIN), bank account, and their tax exempt status. This allows you to focus on running your homeschool group and deal with the IRS paperwork at a later time.

There are pros and cons to a fiscal sponsorship arrangement, so I strongly recommend you do some research and have a formal written agreement. Greg Colvin's book *Fiscal Sponsorship: 6 Ways to Do It Right* and his website http://fiscalsponsorship.com/ are both helpful.

REORGANIZE YOUR GROUP TO STAY SMALL

Another method that avoids IRS filing for tax exempt status would be to reorganize your group to stay under $5,000 gross revenues per year. Your organization could split into separate groups based on their programs or geography. Creating separate groups means that you will have more people serving on leadership boards making the organization more difficult to run efficiently. The new organizations will also need separate checking accounts and their own Employer Identification Numbers (EIN). Each separate organization will be responsible for the required IRS annual information return, The Form 990-N. They may also need to file separate articles of incorporation for nonprofit corporate status in your state. This involves more paperwork and state filing fees.

The extra work of splitting up to stay small may be worthwhile if you think your group is stable and will not continue to grow. If you are like many homeschool groups that continue to add members each year, staying small is not a long term solution.

Pay Taxes

If you are not a tax exempt organization or staying under the $5,000 annual gross revenue limit, then your must pay taxes on any financial surplus. This, obviously, is the least desirable option for homeschool organizations. What taxes you pay and what tax forms you file depend on the business structure of your organization. Your organization may be classified in several ways. A homeschool organization could be a for-profit sole proprietorship, a partnership or a corporation. Additionally, a homeschool group might be a nonprofit corporation that is not tax exempt and therefore should be paying corporate income tax on its surplus.

If your organization is a corporation, you should file a corporate income tax return (IRS Form 1120) and pay taxes at a rate of 15% of your profit (for taxable income under $50,000). Use professional help such as a CPA in preparing your Form 1120 tax return as these returns are quite complicated.

Some homeschool groups are organized as for-profit businesses, usually sole proprietorships or partnerships. These groups would pay income tax on their owners' or partners' individual tax returns. Rates vary from 10-35% of net income.

How To Decide What To Do

Discuss the options with your board. This is an important decision and should not be made by one person alone. Determine the costs and benefits of each option based on your specific group. Some options, like finding a church or fiscal sponsor may not be possible for your group. It is beneficial to make a decision chart listing the pros, cons, costs and benefits of each option. This helps promote an objective view of each option.

Keep the future in mind. The application tax exempt status is a one-time event that will serve your organization well into the future. Once obtained, it is rare for an organization to lose its tax exempt status. There are restrictions and annual reporting requirements, so your leadership should be aware of the responsibilities it is passing to future leaders (See Chapter Ten "We're Tax Exempt! Now What?"). Staying small or paying taxes may not be the best option if your group has plans to grow. Many homeschool organizations find themselves meeting the needs of more families as homeschooling becomes more popular.

Finally, get advice. I cannot encourage this enough. Homeschool leaders should focus on what they do best—running their homeschool program and let the professionals do what they do best—understand the IRS rules! My website http://HomeschoolCPA.com is a good place to start reading and educating yourself and your board. I am also available for individual consultation with your group to help you make this important decision.

[5]

Chapter Five: What Does Your State Require?

A nonprofit organization often has reporting obligations to their state as well as the federal government. At the state level your organization may work with several state agencies including:

- Secretary of State for nonprofit incorporation and name registration
- Attorney General for charity registration
- Department of Revenue for tax exemption

Nonprofit attorneys Hurwit Associates list the filing requirement for nonprofit organizations for each state on their website at http://www.hurwitassociates.com/ .

SECRETARY OF STATE'S OFFICE

If you apply to be a nonprofit corporation, it is usually through the Secretary of State's Office. Additionally, name registrations are filed with the Secretary of State. They act as a record keeper and want to know who is doing business in their state under an assumed name.

Each state is slightly different in their requirement for filing as a nonprofit corporation. The state's goal is to offer nonprofit status only to organizations that have a legitimate charitable purpose. Your organization should have a mission statement that briefly describes your purpose, such as:

> "Our purpose is educational. We provide support to home schooling families with classes, events and activities."

Although some states like Pennsylvania allow an individual to start a nonprofit, a single individual should not start a nonprofit all alone. It should be a team effort. Most states will require an established board of directors of at least three people. Some states do allow an individual to form a nonprofit corporation, but the IRS will expect to see a board of directors running the nonprofit to be eligible for tax exempt status. Choose at least three people to serve as President, Secretary and Treasurer. Five directors is usually recommended.

Application for nonprofit incorporation can usually be found at your Secretary of State's website. Nonprofit attorneys at Hurwit Associates list the websites of each states' Secretary of State offices as well as filing fees. Visit http://www.hurwitassociates.com/

If you plan an applying for 501(c)(3) tax exempt status with the IRS, there is special language that the IRS will expect to see in your Articles of Incorporation filed with your Secretary of State. Without this language (concerning purpose, lobbying limitations and disposition of assets), the IRS will not grant tax exempt status. Your application will be delayed until you refile amended articles with your secretary of state. These delays can be frustrating and expensive.

Often, your secretary of state will not tell you of these IRS requirements because the state does not require the specific language; it is an

IRS requirement. Read Chapter Seven for details on nonprofit incorporation. The Appendix has sample Articles of Incorporation that includes the required IRS language.

ATTORNEY GENERAL'S OFFICE

The state Attorney General's office protects the citizens of the state from crooks and thieves. For this reason, many states require nonprofit organization to register with their state, especially if they conduct fund raising or solicit donations from the public.

Some states want to know if your group is soliciting donations, even if you are not a 501(c)(3) organization or are not a nonprofit corporation. They usually call this notification a Charity Registration. It is usually done through the Attorney General's Office. The Attorney General acts like a sheriff on the look-out for crooks. They want to know who is selling merchandise as a fund raiser and who is asking for donations. The Charity Registration form can be simple or rather complex. It usually requests board members names, dates of the fund raiser, information on how the funds are raised, details on how the funds will be used, and a financial statement every year.

STATE DEPARTMENT OF REVENUE

The state also wants to know if a business exists so it can collect taxes. Many states will exempt nonprofits from state income tax if they have IRS tax exempt status. Sometimes it requires another application, but most states recognize federal tax exemption automatically. Your nonprofit may apply for state tax exemption through the Department of Revenue or through the Secretary of State.

Most states also allow nonprofit organizations to be exempt from sales tax on their purchases. Sales tax exemption is frequently granted through the Department of Revenue. There is usually a form to fill out requesting sales tax exemption on purchases you make related to your exempt purpose.

Note that sales tax exemption does not apply to items you sell. If you are selling books or products to your homeschool members, you may have to collect sales tax from them and remit it to your state. Contact your state department of revenue or research sales tax using their website. Each state is different and some allow nonprofits to sell products for a limited number of days without collecting sales tax.

Chapter Six: 501(c)(3) Status: What Is Involved?

I have mentioned the paperwork, fees and suggestions of legal and accounting advice to establish your group as a tax exempt charitable organization with the Internal Revenue Service (IRS). Before you even begin the application process, your organization will have several tasks including establishing a Board of Directors, creating bylaws and drafting either a constitution or Articles of Incorporation.

ARE YOU READY?

The IRS application for 501(c)(3) tax exempt status can be a daunting task. The IRS designed it that way! According IRS statistics, about 70% of applications for tax exempt status are not granted. This is usually because the applicant drops out of the system, not because the IRS rejects them. The IRS actually approves 99% of applicants who complete the process. Applicants drop out because they decide the process was not worth it. The IRS questions and requests for more data discourage them. Sometimes the organization cannot supply what the

IRS is requesting such as bylaws, board members' names, conflict of interest policies, etc. In order to have success with the 501(c)(3) application, you must be prepared and properly organized.

Here's a check list to see if your organization is ready to apply for 501(3)(3) tax exempt status:

❑ Do you have a mission statement with a clear charitable focus (education is one of the approved charitable categories with the IRS)?

❑ Do you have a board of directors, regular meetings and a method to elect the board?

❑ Do you have bylaws and articles of incorporation or a charter, usually called the organization's governing documents?

❑ Do you keep minutes of your meetings?

❑ Do you have five years of financial history (for existing organizations) or can you estimate two years of future financial statements (for new organizations)?

❑ Would you be willing to forgo any political candidate endorsements? 501(c)(3) organizations may not endorse political candidates.

❑ Do you have enough money to pay the IRS filing fee of $400 or $850?

If you said no to any of these items, you are not ready for 501(c)(3) application. Work to get your board organized and the paperwork ready and the process will go smoothly. The following sections in this book will help you prepare.

WRITING A MISSION STATEMENT

A mission statement is a concise way to state your organization's purpose. It helps focus and clarify the goal of your organization. A mission statement must do two things. It must tell others who you are and it must remind you of what your focus should be both now and in the future.

WHO AND WHAT, BUT NOT HOW

A mission statement answers two questions:

Who are you? Are you defined geographically, by religious affiliation, by age of students, by skills, styles, or by curriculum choice? Who is your target audience? Is it parents, kids, athletic students, musical students, or high school students?

Why do you exist? Is it to encourage parents, support students, offer information, offer opportunities, promote homeschooling or to influence legislation?

A mission statement does not answer the how question ("How do you accomplish your purpose?"). The how question would be a description of your activities, such as: hold classes, run a sports program, organize field trips, etc. The description of your activities should be in another statement called a Program Statement.

TIPS FOR WRITING A MISSION STATEMENT

- Use words like: try, seek, influence, or encourage.
- Keep your mission statement short. Ideally one sentence or about 50 words.
- Be accurate. Do not make your purpose unattainable or sound loftier than you can accomplish. Your organization cannot be all things to all people.
- Put your mission statement everywhere. Put it on letterhead, posters and on a sign at every board meeting.

SAMPLE MISSION STATEMENTS

Here are some sample mission statements to guide you:

"The purpose of this organization shall be to provide support, information and encouragement to homeschooling families."

"This organization serves to teach and disseminate educational materials for the public and to help parents of home schooled children fulfill educational requirements."

"The mission of this homeschool co-op is to provide affordable, quality, fun-filled academic classes to children in the homeschool community."

"We exist to encourage, support and build up a community of Christian homeschool families."

See the Appendices for more Sample Mission Statements.

Establishing a Board of Directors

Forming a board to help in leadership should not be difficult if you seek qualified people, ask them to help with specific duties and form committees for large tasks.

Forming a board

Follow the Biblical example of Moses, who could not handle the burden of leadership alone. God directed Moses to:

> "Bring me seventy of Israel's elders who are known to you as leaders and officials among the people.... They will help you carry the burden of the people so that you will not have to carry it alone." (Numbers 11:16)

You should do the same and establish a Board of Helpers, sometimes called by its more formal name, Board of Directors or Leadership Team. This doesn't have to be formal. Simply, choose people of integrity with gifts of organization and discernment. Look for people who show an interest and commitment to you group. If they have experience in serving on a charitable or church board it would be extremely helpful.

JUST ASK

Approach potential board members personally, emphasize their strengths and contributions to your organization, and ask if they would be willing to help in a leadership role.

KEEP IT SMALL AND FORM COMMITTEES

Keep your board small so decisions can be made easily. Every board should have at least three members: a president, a secretary and a treasurer. Some boards prefer to add a vice president who will succeed the current president.

As responsibilities increase, the size of the board should increase. Most boards assign committees to handle many tasks. Committees meet outside of board meetings. A co-op of 20-100 families might have a board of about four or five members and two to five committees.

IDEAS FOR COMMITTEES

Committees for a homeschool co-op might include these:
- Registration
- Building Use
- Classes & Teachers
- Events
- Financial
- Fund raising

Committees for a homeschool support group might include:
- Membership
- New Member Info & Welcome
- Events & Field Trips

- Legislative Liaison

These are just ideas. Your committees may be different.

DEFINE THE TASK

Keep board member tasks well defined and limited. Some people are reluctant to volunteer for leadership because they fear there is no getting out later! If you define their role specifically and limit the term to one year, they may commit freely.

Delegate to the general membership some duties. Our co-op found it difficult for the director to make morning announcements because she had so many responsibilities at the start of co-op. Our board looked around and noticed that one particular woman was always there on time (or early), had a strong voice and was already organizing field trips. We asked her to take over the job of doing morning announcements for the next semester. We complimented her organizational skills and promptness. She agreed and our director had a huge weight lifted!

WRITING BYLAWS

The IRS will request to see a copy of your bylaws. They are a part of your organizing documents along with your Articles of Incorporation. Sample bylaws and Articles of Incorporation can be found in the Appendices.

THE PURPOSE OF BYLAWS

Bylaws spell out how the organization will operate and they also configure the board of directors. Bylaws specify the organization's rules of internal operation. For example the bylaws specify the number of members of the Board, the length each member serves on the board, the officer positions, and how meetings are conducted. One of the first duties of the board of directors is to write and approve the bylaws.

WHAT TO INCLUDE IN YOUR BYLAWS

Name: The legal name of your organization not its "doing business as" name.

Purpose: Be very specific. Use a mission statement or a Bible verse if desired.

Location: Name your city, county and state

Qualifications of members: Not all homeschool nonprofits have members. Even the word "member" can be loosely defined. Members do not have to be given the right to vote. Sometime it's too cumbersome to get members together for an annual meeting or a vote. Examples of qualifications for membership might include: payment of dues, agreeing to a statement of faith, legally homeschooling according to state laws, or just "homeschooling" or even just "interested in homeschooling."

Meetings: How often will the board meet? Is a quorum required? Is majority vote required? Will proxy votes be allowed? How will the meetings be announced?

Board of Directors and Officers: Will the board be elected by members or self-elected? Will the terms be one year or more?

Position descriptions for President, Vice President, Treasurer and Secretary

Qualifications of board members: Should they be a member of the group for at least a year before serving on the board?

Conflict resolution polices: Include the Biblical standard here if desired or mention general guidelines. If you adopt an official Conflict of Interest policy include it here. See the Appendix for sample Conflict of Interest policies.

Committees: How are committees formed? "At the request of board" is a common clause found in bylaws.

WHAT TO LEAVE OUT OF YOUR BYLAWS

Do not include in your bylaws day-to-day to day operating policies such as:

- Dress codes
- Discipline policies
- Schedules
- Names of officers
- Location of your meeting

These items are subject to frequent changes and should not be in your bylaws.

Bylaws should not be confused with your organization's daily operating policies. Try not to be too specific in your bylaws. I've seen bylaws that mention where meetings take place. Meeting location can change frequently and should not be in the bylaws. A general guideline like "Quarterly meetings shall be held" is more flexible. Leave the details to operating policies. Put all these day-to-day type of items in another document such as a policy manual or an operating handbook.

COPY FROM OTHERS

A good way to start writing your bylaws is to review bylaws of other organizations, including churches. Some nonprofits put their bylaws on their website and you can read them on-line. You could also get advice from a lawyer or accountant familiar with nonprofit organizations to help write your bylaws.

The Appendices of this book have sample bylaws. An electronic copy in Microsoft Word is also available at www.HomeschoolCPA.com under Leader Tools.

[7]

Chapter Seven: Nonprofit Incorporation: Do You Need It?

Establishing a Board of Directors, creating bylaws and planning a budget for home school organizations are important steps toward 501(c)(3) status. Small organizations may not need this level of organization. They can exist with simple guidelines and a collected cash pool. But I believe that as organizations grow they benefit from more structure.

If your organization is continuing to grow, you may need to consider becoming incorporated. In this chapter I'll discuss some confusion about incorporation, the pros and cons and how to know if your organization is ready.

WHAT IS INCORPORATION?

When you started your home school organization you were considered an "unincorporated association." Groups can exist in this form forever. Becoming a corporation means you are establishing a separate legal identity. It means your group can now put "Inc." behind their name. It is sort of like going from "Mom & Pop Store" to "Mom & Pop, Inc."

The business operations may stay the same, but a separate, legal entity has been created. State governments handle the applications for incorporation, usually in the Secretary of State's Office.

INCORPORATING IS NOT THE SAME AS TAX EXEMPT STATUS

Incorporating in your state as a nonprofit corporation does not grant your organization special tax status with the state or federal governments. It does not mean you are automatically tax exempt. Nor does not mean you are a 501(c)(3) charitable organization. 501(c)(3) status is granted by the IRS after an application process.

Incorporating may not even finish your involvement with your state government, either. Most states require you to update your corporation status on a regular basis; some want annual updates while others only expect to hear from you every few years. Additionally, most states require nonprofits to register if they do fund raising or solicit donations from the public. This is usually handled by the state's Attorney General's office, or state tax department. See Chapter Five "What Does Your State Require?" for more details.

DO YOU NEED TO INCORPORATE?

Incorporation allows you to protect your leadership. The corporation, not its leaders, will become liable for any legal or financial problems. The directors of a corporation have limited liability. That means that if your corporation is found to be responsible for an injury or loss, only the assets of the corporation can be taken, not the personal assets of the leaders.

Nonprofit incorporation does not take the place of liability insurance. A nonprofit can be sued, but your members and directors can be protected from personal liability.

Another reason to incorporate is a desire for the organization to exist beyond the current leadership. The establishment of a nonprofit corporation establishes legal entity with bylaws to perpetuate its continued existence. The bylaws spell out how new leaders will be selected or replaced, thus assuring the groups will continue to function if the current leaders step down.

Additionally, many organizations incorporate when they purchase real estate or hire employees. These transactions requirement legal agreements and should be entered into by the corporation instead of individual leaders. In other words, a worker should be paid by Homeschool Group, Inc. and not by the volunteer president or leader of the group.

Many organizations become incorporated as a nonprofit corporation in their state prior to applying for 501(c(3) tax exempt status with the IRS. The IRS will accept an unincorporated association for 501(c)(3) status, but the group would have to reapply of they later became a corporation. Incorporation establishes a new legal entity, so in the eyes of the IRS the old organization was granted tax exempt status, not the newly incorporated organization. To avoid having to reapply for tax exempt status with the IRS, it is best to become a nonprofit corporation first.

WHAT DOES INCORPORATING INVOLVE?

The disadvantages to incorporating are primarily the cost and the paperwork. The paperwork is usually fairly simple. Most states require only a one-page form listing the legal name of the organization and the officers' names. Your Secretary of State's office will have information on incorporating as a nonprofit organization. The fees for incorporating run from $30 to $400. It may take two to six weeks. Visit http://www.hurwitassociates.com to view your state's requirements.

You may want to incorporate by yourself or consult a knowledgeable lawyer or accountant. There are several types of corporations, so choose someone familiar with nonprofit incorporation. You will be paying for their expertise in addition to the fees the state charges.

MEMBERS OR NOT?

Many homeschool organizations file to become nonprofit corporations in their state and the form usually asks: Does your corporation have members? Well, naturally most homeschool groups have members, but the best answer might be "No."

Read the question carefully. It asks if your corporation has members. Your group may have members, but not the corporation. What's the difference? For-profit corporations have shareholders. These shareholders are entitled to a vote on matters brought to their attention. A nonprofit corporation may have members, but is not required to have members. If a nonprofit corporation has members, then those members are entitled to a vote on matters brought to them. Typically, this might be electing board members, approving the budget, choosing to hire paid staff, etc. (the bylaws usually spell out what members vote on).

> Voting memberships are useful when an organization wishes to be democratically controlled by its constituents. Voting memberships structures are commonly used by member driven organizations such as social clubs, churches, chambers of commerce and trade associations. In such cases, the organization exists to serve its members and it makes sense for control to be vested in the members. [11]

Some nonprofit corporations do not have members; instead decisions are made by the board. The members do not have a vote, nor do they elect board members. The board appoints replacement board members (it's called self-perpetuating). Many homeschool organizations may have members participating in their activities (co-op classes, filed trips, clubs, etc.), but not have voting members of the corporation. Instead, they have a board that makes the decisions.

Advantages of a board-run organization (i.e., no members of the corporation)

- A board-run homeschool group does not have to gather members together for a vote.
- Decisions can be made more quickly.
- A smaller group of people, the board, makes the decisions

Disadvantages of a board-run organization (i.e., no members of the corporation)

- No input from the members.
- The board replaces itself and could become insular with no new ideas.

If your Articles of Incorporation state you have members, but you want to change that, you will have to amend the Articles of Incorporation. This will probably take a vote of the members. State law dictates who can change the form of the corporation. It usually involves holding a member meeting to change the Articles of Incorporation, filing some paperwork with your state and paying a small fee to your state (typically $30-$50).

Tax Exempt Provisions in Articles of Incorporation

Although your state may not request a copy, your organization should write Articles of Incorporation. The IRS will want to see a copy when you apply for tax exempt status. Your Articles of Incorporation are a legal record of the name, address and purpose of your organization. Think of it as a birth announcement for your organization. If Articles of Incorporation are a birth announcement, then bylaws are the parenting handbook.

A word of caution: If you plan an applying for 501(c)(3) tax exempt status with the IRS, there is special language of about four paragraphs that the IRS will expect to see in your Articles of Incorporation filed with your Secretary of State. Without this language (concerning purpose, lobbying limitations and disposition of assets), the IRS will not grant tax exempt status. Your application will be delayed until you re-file amended articles with your secretary of state. These delays can be frustrating and expensive.

Often, your secretary of state will not tell you of these IRS requirements because the state does not require the specific language; it is an IRS requirement. The Appendix has sample Articles of Incorporation that includes the required IRS language.

Here is what the IRS requires in your Articles of Incorporation:

_____ is organized exclusively for charitable, religious, educational, and/or scientific purposes under section 501(c)(3) of the Internal Revenue Code. No part of the net earnings of _____ net earnings shall inure to the benefit of, or be distributable to its members, trustees, officers, or other private persons, except that the organization shall be authorized and empowered to pay reasonable compensation for services rendered and to make payments and distributions in furtherance of the purposes set forth in the purpose clause hereof.

No substantial part of the activities of _____ shall be the carrying on of propaganda, or otherwise attempting to influence legislation, and the organization shall not participate in, or intervene in (including the publishing or distribution of statements) any political campaign on behalf of any candidate for public office.

Upon the dissolution of _____, assets shall be distributed for one or more exempt purposes within the meaning of section 501(c)(3) of the

Internal Revenue Code, or corresponding section of any future federal tax code, or shall be distributed to the federal government, or to a state or local government, for public purpose.

Notwithstanding any other provision of this document, the organization shall not carry on any other activities not permitted to be carried on (a) by an organization exempt from federal income tax under section 501(c)(3) of the Internal Revenue Code, or corresponding section of any future federal tax code, or (b) by an organization, contributions to which are deductible under section 170(c)(2) of the Internal Revenue Code, or corresponding section of any future federal tax code.

These required paragraphs must be included in your Articles of Incorporation, not just in your bylaws. Bylaws are subject to change quite easily, usually by a simple vote of the board. The IRS is looking for more permanence than that. These provisions should be part of your organizing documents and not easy to alter. Feel free to repeat them in your bylaws, because it is more likely your future board members will read your bylaws than your Articles of Incorporation.

CHOOSING YOUR NAME CAREFULLY

Your organization will probably have at least two names You may have a legal name that is different from your "doing business as" (DBA) name. For legal purposes, a name should be very distinct, so your group will not be confused with another group or confused with a school. My co-op's legal name is "Mason Ohio Educational Home School Organization." Quite a mouthful, huh? We're called "Mason Home School Co-op" on our checking account and "Mason Co-op" to members. Why the difference? In the state of Ohio, use of the word "co-op" in your name is reserved for corporations who file under the Cooperative Corporation Law. The name "co-op" can be used by any organization if you follow Ohio's law's for co-ops. These usually apply to electric co-ops or rural co-ops and involve things like sharing profits, membership voting, etc. We don't want to follow those guidelines, so we cannot use the word "co-op." We avoided the word "co-op" in our legal name. In our "DBA" name we use it.

SEVEN GREAT REASONS TO INCORPORATE

Does your homeschool organization need to incorporate? Here's a short quiz to see if incorporating in your state as a nonprofit organization would be beneficial. Answering "Yes" to any one of these questions is enough reason to become a nonprofit corporation.

Do you consistently make a financial surplus (i.e. a profit)? Incorporate as a nonprofit and then apply for tax exempt status with the IRS.

Do you wish to legally and financially protect your leadership? Incorporate as a nonprofit so you can legally protect your leaders. A nonprofit can be sued, but your members and directors can be protected from personal liability of they are not guilty of fraud or gross negligence.

Do you wish the organization to last beyond the current leadership? Incorporate so your organization has a legal identity of its own and will exist even after current leadership leaves.

Do you wish to hire employees or purchase property or equipment? Incorporate so the organization pays employees or owns the property, not individuals. Also, nonprofits may be exempt from paying property taxes on real estate and other property. Contact your county assessor's office for more information on property tax exemption.

Do you have donors who want a tax deduction for their donations? Incorporate with your state as a nonprofit and then pursue the 501(c)(3) charitable status with the IRS.

Do you expect to receive private or public grant money? Your group is unlikely to qualify for many public and private grants without 501(c)(3) status.

Do you do a lot of bulk mailing? Nonprofits can receive a mailing permit that gives them a special reduced nonprofit rate for mailings. This is helpful for organizations that will do a lot of mailings. The post office may request to see Articles of Incorporation and bylaws.

Becoming a nonprofit corporation may be in your organization's future. There are fees and paperwork involved, but there are benefits, especially if you have a financial surplus, wish to have a separate legal identity and protect your leadership.

[8]

Chapter Eight: Checklist for Homeschool Organizations Seeking 501(c)(3) Status

INITIAL SET UP

- ❑ Choose a board of directors (often only three people are needed, a president/director, a treasurer and secretary). More is usually better including a vice-chair/director.
- ❑ Choose a name for your nonprofit. Research the IRS Charities web site (www.irs.gov/eo), the internet and your state's Secretary of State's Office to be sure it is not already taken.
- ❑ Develop organizational bylaws—the rules by which you will operate. See a sample at http://HomeschoolCPA.com under Leader Tools/Sample Documents.
- ❑ Read the articles on nonprofit incorporation at http://homeschoolcpa.com/leader-tools/articles/
- ❑ Hold your first board meeting. Get approval of the bylaws and discuss the decision to form a nonprofit corporation.

- ❑ Draft Articles of Incorporation including a statement of your purpose and the IRS required language concerning private benefit and inurement, political activities, and distribution of assets upon dissolution. See a sample at http://HomeschoolCPA.com under Leader Tools/Sample Documents.

- ❑ Incorporate as a nonprofit organization in your state. Submit Articles of Incorporation to the appropriate office in your state government with the required fee. This is usually the Secretary of State's Office.

- ❑ Obtain a Federal Employer Identification Number (EIN) by submitting IRS Form SS-4 (visit www.IRS.gov and search for "EIN") using the legal name of your new nonprofit corporation.

- ❑ Set up a budget for the current year and projections for two future years (if you are a new organization) or gather financial data for five prior years if you are an existing organization.

BEGIN 501(C)(3) APPLICATION

- ❑ Have your board vote to approve filing for 501(c)(3) tax exempt status. Approve the expenditure of funds to pay the IRS fee ($850 if gross annual revenues are greater than $10,000, or $400 if gross annual revenue is less than $10,000) and any professional fees.

- ❑ Determine your eligibility to file using the shorter Form 1023-EZ. The IRS Eligibility checklist is found in the instructions to the Form 1023-EZ available here: http://www.irs.gov/pub/irs-pdf/i1023ez.pdf . If you need help determining your eligibility, contact http://HomeschoolCPA.com.

❑ If you are not eligible for the Form 1023-EZ, begin writing your Narrative (Part IV) explaining who you are, what you do, your history and reason for wanting tax exempt status.

❑ Fill in the financial sections and other parts of the Form 1023.

❑ Have your board review the Form 1023 and sign where indicated. (Carol Topp, CPA can also review your self-prepared application. Contact her at http://HomeschoolCPA.com for details.)

❑ Mail to IRS with the appropriate fee of $850 if gross annual revenues are greater than $10,000, or $400 if gross annual revenue is less than $10,000

AFTER THE APPLICATION IS FILED

❑ Expect a confirmation letter from the IRS in 10-14 days indicating they received the application.

❑ Reply promptly if the IRS has any questions or needs additional information.

❑ Receive the IRS determination letter and celebrate! Make copies of the letter and keep in several safe places.

YOU'RE TAX EXEMPT!

❑ Read IRS Publication 4221 Compliance Guide for 501(c)(3) Charities available to http://IRS.gov . Discuss your record keeping and reporting requirements with your board.

❑ Register as a charity within your state if you are required. Several states do not require registration unless you solicit the public in a fund raising event.

❑ File your annual Form 990-N, 990-EZ or 990 as required.

[9]

Chapter Nine: The Application Process

The Internal Revenue Service (IRS) application for tax exempt status, Form 1023, is a 28 page document. The IRS estimates 70 hours to complete Form 1023. The new (as of July 2014), shorter Form 1023-EZ is only two-and-a half pages long, but several of the questions are worded in a way that can be very confusing to someone unfamiliar with the IRS jargon and tax exempt law.

You can fill out the Form 1023 or 1023-EZ by yourself or hire a knowledgeable professional to assist you. There are lawyers and accountants that will file Form 1023 for you. Naturally, I hope you choose me if you hire a professional. Remember that in addition to being affordable, HomeschoolCPA is the only service that specializes in homeschooling organizations. I understand homeschool groups and what they are doing, so I can best represent you to the IRS. HomeschoolCPA is also one of the few services that will also assist you in filing your annual information return to the IRS (Form 990). Other services will help you get tax exempt status, but not help you maintain it!

If you do decide to go it alone, I highly recommend you spend a little money and buy some helpful resources. I recommend Sandy Deja's ebook Prepare Your Own 501(c)(3) Application available at http://www.form1023help.com

The IRS's latest Form 1023 is available at www.IRS.gov . Search for "Form 1023." It's available as a fill-in form, so no special software is needed to fill in the application. The Form 1023-EZ is filed online at Pay.gov, but I recommend you look over the form before attempting to prepare it online. The form can be viewed (but not filed) here: http://www.irs.gov/pub/irs-pdf/f1023ez.pdf .

TIPS FOR IRS FORM 1023

Do not fill in by hand. Use the IRS fill-in form on-line. You can save it on your computer.

Answer every question even if you put N/A for Not Applicable.

If you need extra space for additional information, attach paper at the end of the application.

Always include your organization's name and EIN at the top of the page.

Avoid using words like scholarship when you mean fee reduction.

Avoid the word "co-op". Many states have a cooperative incorporation statutes. The word co-op cannot be used in your organization's name unless you are incorporated under these statutes. If you want to use the word co-op, explain its use to the IRS. (See the Chapter Seven)

Avoid calling yourself a school or checking the box in Part X, Line 5b indicating you are a school. Most homeschool co-ops do not fit the IRS's description of a school (regularly schedule curriculum, regular, qualified faculty and enrolled student body, and facilities). Instead they usually fit Line 5h that describes an organization supported by membership fees or income from "activities related to its exempt purpose."

I won't go into details about the Form 1023 here, but I will offer suggestions on a few key areas, namely your narrative, your board and governing documents, and financial records.

Your Narrative

In Part IV of the Form 1023, the IRS is looking for a detailed narrative about your organization. This is the heart of the application. Begin the narrative with the statement, "We are an educational organization formed specifically to..." and then launch into your mission statement.

The Narrative should be at least one page or more. Include a history of your organization, specific activities, number of participants, how you are managed and funded, and why you seek tax exemption.

A Board and Bylaws

Part V of the Form 1023 addresses your board and their compensation. It is not typical for nonprofit board members to be compensated. Most board members volunteer their efforts because they feel a passion for the mission. Sometimes homeschooling organizations offer reduced fees or tuition for board members. This is a form of compensation that should be mentioned on your application. If the reduced fee or tuition is reasonable and in recognition for services rendered, the IRS will not object.

Financial Statements

The IRS Form 1023 requests two financial statements in Part IX, Statement of Revenue and Expenses and a Balance Sheet. The IRS provides forms with pre-selected categories. These may or may not fit your organization's financial categories. You can use the IRS forms or you can supply your own financial statements.

If you use your own reporting form I highly recommend you get a CPA to examine your financial data. You do not need fully audited financial statements, but please seek advice about the presentation of your financial data if you prepare the Form 1023 yourself. I provide an examination of your self-prepared Form 1023 including the financial statements. See www.HomeschoolCPA.com for details.

The IRS accepts historical data if you are an existing organization or projected financial data if you are a new organization. Do not have gaps in your data. Here is a sample of what a homeschool organization's Statement of Revenue and Expenses might look like, followed by a Balance Sheet. Your specific categories may vary.

	Current Year	5 Prior Years or 2 future years		
	From ____ to	From ____ to	From ____ to	From ____ to

Revenue

Gifts and Contributions				
Revenue from running your programs				
"Tuition" or class fees				
Sale of merchandise				
Other: (Please describe)				
Membership dues or fees				
Investment Income (Interest)				
Unusual Grants				
Fundraisers(please describe)				
Other Revenue (describe)				

Total Revenue

Expenses

Fundraising expenses(describe)				
Compensation of Director or Officers				
Other Salaries and wages				
Rent & Utilities				
Professional fees				
Expenses related to your program				
Supplies				
Teacher pay (as Independent Contractors)				
Appreciation Awards				
Office expense				
Advertising (& web site)				
Insurance				
Other Program expenses (describe)				
Other Expenses				

Total Expenses

Balance Sheet   Year End:

Assets

Cash
Accounts Receivable
Inventory
Investments (attach list)
Depreciable assets (attach a list)
Land
Other assets (attach list)
                                    Total Assets

Liabilities

Accounts Payable
Gifts or Grants Payable
Mortgages or loans payable (attach list)
Other liabilities
                                    Total Liabilities

Fund Balances or Net Assets

Total Fund Balances or Net Assets (line 16 less line 11)
        Total Liabilities and Fund Balances (add lines 16 and 17)

If you need assistance is recording your financial data, please see my book *Money Management in a Homeschool Organization* available at www.HomeschoolCPA.com .

[10]

Chapter Ten: We're Tax Exempt! Now What?

Now that you have received tax exempt status, your work isn't finished. Maintaining your tax exempt status is an important job. Fortunately, it isn't difficult to safeguard your 501(c)(3) status if you follow a few rules. These rules involve annual reporting to the IRS and your state, limiting political involvement, making proper disclosures to donors, and avoiding conflicts of interest and excess benefits.

ANNUAL REPORTING TO THE IRS AND YOUR STATE

FORM 990

Tax exempt organizations with annual gross receipts over $50,000 must file a Form 990 with the IRS annually. The Form 990, officially called Return of Organization Exempt from Income Tax, is not a tax return. Tax exempt organizations do not usually pay income tax. They may still pay employer tax like Social Security, or income tax on revenue from a business not related to their tax exempt function. Call your annual reporting "the 990," not "our tax return." The 990 is really an information return.

Gross receipts include everything your organization receives as income, even if it is spent almost immediately.

SMALL NONPROFITS FILE AN ANNUAL ELECTRONIC POSTCARD

If your organization normally receives less than $50,000 in gross revenue in a year, you don't have to file a Form 990 at all. Instead, small organizations will file an annual "notice," Form 990-N, called an electronic postcard. The 990-N confirms an organization's continued existence, current address, and gross revenues. For more information visit the IRS website, www.IRS.gov and search on "Form 990-N"

The IRS will allow an organization to average the past three years gross receipts (including the year for which calculations are being made) to determine if the $50,000 threshold has been passed. This allows an organization to have one unusual year of higher than expected income and still file the simpler 990-N.

990-EZ

There is a simplified Form 990 called 990-EZ. Organizations with gross revenues under $200,000 (and assets under $500,000) can use the 990-EZ. This will apply to many homeschool organizations.

DUE DATE

The Form 990 (or 990-N or 990-EZ) is due on the 15th day of the fifth month after the end of your fiscal year. Some homeschool groups run on a calendar year, so their year ends December 31. Their Form 990 would be due May 15. Many homeschool groups run on a "school year" basis and may have a fiscal year end of June 30th. Their Form 990 would be due November 15. You can request an automatic three month extension. Automatic means it will automatically be approved without giving a reason. Use IRS Form 8868 to request an extension.

FAILURE TO FILE FORM 990

If your organization fails to file their annual information return with the IRS (Form 990, 990-EZ or 990-N) for three consecutive years, your tax exempt status is automatically revoked. This is a serious loss because your organization may not receive tax deductible donations and pay owe income tax during the period that you are not tax exempt. Fortunately, the IRS has created a streamlined process to get your tax exempt status reinstated. It involves paperwork and some fees, but does not usually involve penalties or back taxes. Read Chapter 11 for more information about getting your tax exempt status reinstated.

UNRELATED BUSINESS INCOME TAX

A homeschool group, like many charities, may bring in revenues from fund raising. These efforts can be so successful that leaders may wonder if your group owes anything to the government in taxes. For the most part, fund raising is not considered part of your group's mission; it is just a means to the end. After all, your group's mission is to encourage homeschooling or education, not to sell ads, pizza or other products.

The Internal Revenue Service calls the money you raise "Unrelated Business Income," meaning it is money collected in a trade or business that is not related to your primary mission or what the IRS calls your "exempt purpose." The IRS assess a tax on unrelated business income called the Unrelated Business Income Tax or UBIT. The purpose of this tax is to prevent nonprofit, tax-exempt organizations from having an unfair advantage over the for-profit marketplace.

The best example of unrelated business income is a gift shop in a nonprofit hospital. The income from a gift shop is not related to the hospital's primary purpose of giving medical treatment, so the profits from the gift shop are taxed. Your homeschool organization could have unrelated business income if you sell T-shirts, candy bars, entertainment books, candles, pizza coupons and a host of other products or if you make money from ads or Amazon commissions on your website.

Fortunately the IRS has several exceptions to paying the UBIT tax:

- A $1,000 threshold allows that the first $1,000 in profit from an unrelated business will not be taxed.
- If the fundraiser (or unrelated business) is run by volunteer efforts (i.e., no paid staff) then the proceeds are not taxed.
- If the fundraiser is not regularly carried on, such as a once-a-year spaghetti supper, then the proceeds are not subject to UBIT.
- If you are selling donated items, like in a garage sale, the income raised is not taxed.

One of these exceptions are bound to apply to most homeschool organizations. The rules regarding UBIT are complex. You can read more about UBIT in IRS Publication 598 Tax on Unrelated Business Income of Exempt Organizations (http://www.irs.gov/pub/irs-pdf/p598.pdf).

STATE REQUIREMENTS

Your state may require reporting on an annual basis. Fortunately many states will accept the federal Form 990. Check with your state for their specific requirements. Here is a helpful website that lists reporting requirements by state. http://www.hurwitassociates.com/ Look under State-by-State Requirements on the left sidebar. Call your state government if the requirements are unclear.

GETTING HELP

The Form 990 is a not a simple form to fill out. It is 12 pages of financial reporting and many questions. Even the shorter 990-EZ is 4 pages long. There are at least a dozen attached schedules that run from one to four pages each. It is more complicated than filling out your personal tax return. Some CPAs and tax preparers consider the Form 990 more difficult to complete than a corporate income tax return. Here are some tips:

- Get help, especially on your first 990. Many CPAs can help in filing out the Form 990, but I recommend an experienced CPA who regularly prepares nonprofit returns. Your local tax preparer may know personal income tax pretty well, but may not be familiar with nonprofit returns.
- Use software. The Urban Institute offers a free on-line version of Form 990. Visit http://efile.form990.org/
- Hire a qualified CPA to review your 990 periodically. Even if you've been filing in the 990 yourself, rules change, so it is a good idea to get a review of your return every few years.
- Read one of several helpful guides to preparing your 990.
- Quality 990 is a helpful site with a goal to improve the reporting of Form 990. www.qual990.org.
- *990 Handbook* or *IRS Form 990:Tax Preparation Guide for Nonprofits* both by Jody Blazek.

Naturally, HomeschoolCPA is here to help. Please visit my website for latest prices and packages that I offer (www.HomeschoolCPA.com). I keep up with the latest changes to the 990, attend workshops, and read several reference books every year. I encourage homeschool groups to focus on what they do best, run their programs, and let the professionals do what they know best, in this case, filing out IRS forms.

DISCLOSURE REQUIREMENTS

Tax exempt organizations must make available for public inspection its exemption application (Form 1023) and its annual return

(Form 990). If a request is made in person, copies must be made available immediately. If the request comes in written form, you need to supply a copy with in 30 days. Some organizations put their 990 on their website. It is a public document for everyone to see. You should not be intimidated by this disclosure. You have great mission – to help homeschooling families and a story to tell. Your Form 990 allows your homeschool organization to shine.

You do not have to make public the list of donors. Only the IRS knows about them. You do not have to make public board minutes or employee salary information either.

DONATIONS

The IRS requires that donors obtain a written acknowledgment of any single contribution over $250. As the charitable organization, you should be ready to give donors a written acknowledgment of their generous donation. Many organizations give a written acknowledgment in the form of a thank you letter for all donations, no matter what the amount.

The IRS also requires the charity to disclose to a donor if a portion of their gift was partly for goods and services given. Perhaps you sell a book for $10, but the donor makes a gift of $15; the $5 difference would be considered a donation. You should show that on your donor receipt. You may have seen statements such as:

"No goods of services were provided in exchange for this gift."

or

"If goods or services were provided to you, the nondeductible portion is shown"

Use these statements on your written acknowledgments to your donors. You can read IRS Publication 1771, Charitable Contributions-Substantiation and Disclosure Requirements for more information.

POLITICAL LIMITATIONS

The IRS says, "501(c)(3) charitable organizations may not intervene in political campaigns or conduct substantial lobbying activities." This means your organization cannot support or endorse a candidate for office, but your group may lobby for or against legislation. Keep your lobbying expenditures "insubstantial," which the IRS defines as less that 5% of your budget.

Homeschool leaders can certainly exercise their rights and be politically active, but those activities need to be kept separated from their tax exempt organization. Leaders should not support candidates in your group's publications or at events. In addition, if your group wishes to invite candidates to speak, they must provide an equal opportunity to their opponent. There should be no show of support or endorsement. Groups can lose their tax exempt status over supporting candidates for office.

If you need more information on this subject, visit the IRS site, www.IRS.gov , and search on "political campaign charities." You will find links to details on the IRS rules concerning political involvement by charities.

CONFLICT OF INTEREST

A conflict of interest may arise in your group if you consider a financial or business arrangement that may benefit one of your leaders.

The IRS has been encouraging use of Conflict of Interest policies lately because some nonprofits were guilty of "excess benefit" payments to board members. Rarely do I find this an issue with home-schooling boards. They do not usually compensate board members, let alone pay them "excessively." Never the less, the goal should be to be above reproach in everything, so here are a few guidelines:

Before you enter into a transaction or business deal, obtain a few of quotes. Perhaps you'd like to hire a board member's husband who is a qualified attorney to consult with your leadership on legal matters, but talk to a few other lawyers before hiring him.

Board members should disclose when they might have a financial interest in a business transaction. They should then refrain from voting on the issue. For example, say your group wants to publish a yearbook and one of the leaders has a printing business. She should tell the board about her business and step out of the room during the decision-making process on which printer to use.

In the Appendix, I have some sample Conflict of Interest policies for your group to consider. The IRS has a suggested policy. Some of these policies are designed for large nonprofits with lots of money in their budgets. Chose a simple policy your organization can live with.

[11]

Chapter Eleven: Tax Exempt Status Revoked

Tax exempt status is rarely revoked by the IRS, but it can happen. Sometimes nonprofit organizations lose their tax exempt status for engaging in activities that are forbidden such as a 501(c)(3) organization endorsing a candidate or distributing its revenues to its board members (called inurement). But, by far the most common way organizations lose their tax exempt status is by automatic revocation for failing to file an information return for three consecutive years.

HISTORY OF AUTOMATIC REVOCATION OF TAX EXEMPT STATUS

For many years the IRS had a problem: nonprofit organizations were not submitting their annual information returns (Form 990 or Form 990-EZ). The IRS let small organizations (under $25,000 per year was considered small) get by without doing any annual filings, but the IRS could not determine if an organization failed to file an annual return because:

1. The organization had closed or

2. The organization had less than $25,000 in income and wasn't required to file a return or

3. The organization was large and just not filing a return with the IRS. In other words, these organizations were not filing the required forms and the IRS didn't like that!

The IRS believed many active nonprofits are not following the reporting rules and complained to Congress who passed the Pension Protection Act in 2006. It required two things from nonprofits:

1. All small organizations (with annual revenues of less than $25,000 at the time; the threshold has now been increased to $50,000) had to start filing an electronic form to the IRS every year. IRS created a new form, called the 990-N or the "e-postcard."

2. All tax-exempt organizations that didn't file an information return for three consecutive years will automatically lose their tax-exempt status.

So 2007, 2008, and 2009 were the first years that the annual notification requirement was in place. In 2010 the first automatic revocations took place. Approximately 275,000 organizations lost their tax exempt status that year—about 16% of the entire nonprofit sector.[12]

Word about the new required annual filing has been slow to get out. After all the IRS doesn't have a big marketing budget. They sent letters, created press releases and even created a YouTube video, but a lot of small nonprofits were still in the dark. Slowly, small organizations learned that their tax exempt status had been automatically revoked and many didn't even know about it! Eventually (in 2014, eight years after Congress created the automatic revocation), the IRS created a streamlined process where small nonprofits could get their tax exempt status reinstated. It's explained in IRS Revenue Procedure 2014-11.

AUTOMATIC REVOCATION

As explained in Chapter 10, the IRS requires an annual information return, Form 990, 990-EZ or 990-N, from all tax exempt organizations. Failure to file an information return for three consecutive years results in automatic revocation of the group's tax exempt status.

In 2010, the IRS has begun revoking the tax-exempt status of non-profit organizations that failed to file a Form 990/990-EZ or 990-N for three years. A large number of these organizations were small non-profits that were not required to file an annual Form 990 because their gross revenues were $50,000 or less and many didn't know about the new IRS requirement.

If your organization has not filed any of the 990/990-EZ/990-N forms for three years, it is likely your tax exempt status was revoked—even without your knowledge.

The IRS may have sent a letter called a CP120. If you received that letter, do not ignore it. You should follow the IRS instructions in the letter to get your tax exempt status reinstated. If you apply for reinstatement in a timely manner (usually within 15 months), you can use the IRS's streamlined reinstatement process. It is a rather simple process, if you do not delay. If you delay replying to the IRS, the reinstatement process will involve significantly more paperwork including filing the missed Form 990s from the past. Read IRS Revenue Procedure 2014-11 to see what paperwork you need to file with the IRS to get your tax exempt status reinstated.

WHAT TO DO IF YOU DID NOT RECEIVE A LETTER FROM THE IRS

You may not have not received a letter because your address has changed or your organization is not in the IRS exempt organizations database. This is true for thousands of tiny organizations or clubs that were not required to file a Form 1023 or 1024 application to be tax exempt. You can search the IRS Select Check database at http://www.irs.gov/Charities-&-Non-Profits/Exempt-Organizations-Select-Check to determine if your organization is on the revoked list.

If you don't find your nonprofit's name on the revoked list, you could call the IRS Customer Service for exempt organizations at 877-829-5500. Give them your name and Employer Identification Number (EIN). Call early in the morning (7:30 or 8:00 am ET) for shortest wait times. Ask what the procedure should be to get reinstated.

How to Get Your Tax Exempt Status Back

If you learn that your tax exempt status has been revoked, don't panic. It can be reinstated, usually back to the date of revocation. The IRS offers several options depending on the organizations size (in dollars) and the length of time that has passed. Nonprofits that reapply for tax exempt status within 15 months of when tax exempt status was revoked, find the reinstatement process easiest.

Getting your tax exempt status involves:

- Filing the Form 1023, 1023-EZ or 1024 application
- Paying the appropriate fee of $400 or $850
- Include a statement giving a "reasonable cause" why your organization failed to file the information returns
- File the missing annual returns
- Include with the application a statement that the missing annual reports have been filed.

IRS penalties will be waived if the organization meets the 5 requirements and is retroactively reinstated.

The reinstatement process can be more complex than the original application for tax exempt status. There are several options and forms to be prepared. Please seek professional help from an experienced Certified Public Accountant. I have assisted several nonprofit organizations in getting their tax exempt status reinstated. Please visit <u>HomeschoolCPA.com</u> for details on my services or to request a phone consultation.

[12]

Chapter Twelve: Resources

My website www.HomeschoolCPA.com is specifically for homeschool nonprofit organizations. It has books, videos, articles, links, and blog posts all to help you run your nonprofit organization.

Nonprofit Kit for Dummies by Stan Hutton and Frances Phillips

How to Form a Nonprofit Corporation by Anthony Mancuso

The IRS has two helpful booklets available on the IRS web site at: www.irs.gov/eo
"Applying for the 501(c)(3) Tax-exempt Status" (Publication 4220)
"Compliance for 501(c)(3) Tax-exempt Organizations" (Publication 4221).

Get Ready Get Set: What Your Need to Know Before Starting a Nonprofit is a free down-loadable book from California Management Assistance Partnership. Visit their website at www.cnmsocal.org and search under Resources and Tools/Starting a Nonprofit.

Prepare Your Own 501(c)(3) Application is an excellent e-book by Sandy Deja, who worked in the Exempt Organization department of the IRS is available at http://www.form1023help.com .

The Urban Institute offers a free on-line program to file Form 990 and 990-EZ at http://efile.form990.org/

File the Form 990-N , the IRS electronic postcard at http://epostcard.form990.org

File the Form 1023-EZ Streamlined Application for Recognition of Exemption Under Section 501(c)(3) at http://Pay.gov .

Quality 990 is a helpful site with a goal to improve the reporting of Form 990. www.qual990.org

990 Handbook and *IRS Form 990:Tax Preparation Guide for Nonprofits* both by Jody Blazek

State-by-State Requirements for nonprofit organizations http://www.hurwitassociates.com/ Click on Areas of Practice. On the left column you can search on State-by-State: Filings, Compliance and Statutes.

Appendices

I. SAMPLE MISSION STATEMENTS

I have read many mission statements from homeschool groups. Here are samples of several. I have included some excellent examples and some you shouldn't copy. *My comments are in italics.* Some names have been altered to protect the guilty!

A WESTERN STATE HOMESCHOOL NETWORK

Mission Statement: _____ Home School Network is an inclusive, statewide home schooling organization serving families across a diverse spectrum of home schooling styles and philosophies. _____ Home School Network exists to protect the fundamental right of the family to educate its children in the manner it deems appropriate without regulation or interference by federal, state or local agencies. _____ Home School Network monitors and responds to legislation, which may pose a threat to home schooling, and to this end, maintains dialog with local, state, and national homeschooling organizations. _____ Home School Network serves to inform and empower home schooling families, educate the public, and foster community among home educators in the state of_____.

Programs: _____ reaches thousands of parents each year through our monthly newsletter, ___News, our Local Contact system, an 800# information line, several publications, including a book, The _____ Homeschool Guide, Homeschooling Your Family Seminars presented throughout the state, Legislative Monitoring Committee, an informative website, and a statewide family homeschooling conference.

Excellent, thorough mission statement and program listing. A mission statement does not have to be this long.

CHRISTIAN HOME EDUCATORS NETWORK, INC.

Mission: The primary purpose of our 1,400 family members is to provide support to each other in efforts to homeschool our children.

Programs: Conferences provide outside speakers with expertise and insight ideas on how too effectively homeschool children. Sports provide physical education activity for fun and group participation. Testing provides a nationally recognized means to test and evaluate our children's scholastic ability.

Excellent! Very nice, clear and concise.

XXX CHRISTIAN HOMESCHOOL CENTER INC

Programs: _____ has operated as an institution which serves to teach and disseminate educational materials for the public and to help parents of home schooled children fulfill (our state) educational requirements

No Mission Statement. This purpose statement sounds more like a mission statement and there is no list of programs.

XXX HOMESCHOOL ORGANIZATION

Mission: Help parents educate own children

Programs: Newsletter on events and resources of interest to homeschool parents and others. approx. 10,000 recipients Support/liaison. network linking homeschooling parents with various entities, public and private and technical resource providers.

Short and sweet.

WEST SIDE HOME EDUCATORS

Mission: The main focus of West Side Home Educators is to provide opportunities for home schooling families to interact with each other through educational and social activities, field trips, and sports.

Programs: We meet weekly (every Wednesday noon-2) in _____ Park, from September through May. Other activities are planned on a monthly basis. The type of events and number of activities are directly related to membership involvement. Parents plan and conduct all activities.

The mission statement is clear and concise. The program section should not list dates or time. They can change frequently.

CHRISTIAN HOME EDUCATION ASSOCIATION OF A SOUTHERN REGION

Mission: Homeschool programs, continuing education

Programs: Annual book fair and conferences serving approximately 1500 parents vendors & speakers presenting workshops for parent support and education - open to the public. Communications to approx. 600 families & surrounding groups via website, newsletter, information packets & other mailings and telephone/email of info regarding regional issues. Meetings throughout the year for parents' continuing education and leadership teaching.

Good list of programs, but an unclear mission statement

XXX ACADEMIC LEAGUE

Mission: _____ Academic League is a membership-based coalition of parents and others who have banded together for the furtherance of educational excellence through alternatives to the government operated public schools.

Programs: _____ Academic League sponsors activities that include regional Science Olympiad and Math Counts.

Good mission statement and a clear, but brief, list of programs offered.

II. Sample Bylaws

Here is a sample bylaws that I find very suitable for homeschool groups. Comments are in italics. Delete the italic comments when you write your own bylaws. Feel free to alter the titles used. If you like Leadership Team better than Board of Directors, use it. This document refers to Directors, but you may substitute the title "board members" or even "leaders" if you wish. This document is available in Microsoft Word format at www.HomeschoolCPA.com for easy editing.

Sample Bylaws for a Homeschool Nonprofit

Article 1 – Name, Purpose, Location

Section 1 – The name of this organization shall be _____.

Section 2 – ____ is organized exclusively for educational purposes under section 501(c)(3) of the Internal Revenue Code The mission of _____ is to _____

Section 3 – The principle office location of _____ shall be located in _____ County in the State of ___ . The organization may have any number of offices at such places as the Board may determine.

Article 2 – Membership

(Your group does not have to have members. You can simply state here that "This organization has no members." Or if the board is the full membership, then say "The membership consists of the Board of Directors")

Section 1 – The qualification for membership in this organization are: _____*(Qualifications can be payment of dues, legally homeschooling and/or signing a statement of faith)*

Section 2 - Membership to the organization is fee-based, requiring dues. (Obviously an optional statement. Include it if it is true)

Section 3 – Members of the organization shall have the right to one vote on matters submitted to a vote of the membership including election of officers. (Modify this statement as your group sees fit. Some homeschool groups have members, but members have no voting rights.)

Article 3 – Meetings

Section 1 – The date of the regular annual meeting shall be determined by the Board of Directors who will also set the time and place.

Section 2 – Regular meetings of the Board may be held at such place and time as shall be designated by the standing resolution of the Board.

Section 3 – Special meetings may be called by _____. (*Who? The Chair, any officer, Exec Director*)

Section 4 – Notice of all meetings shall be provided to each voting member, by _____, (*mail, fax, email , any and all methods*) at least ____ weeks/days prior to the meeting.

Article 4 – Board of Directors

Section 1 – The business of the organization shall be managed by a Board of Directors comprised of at least ___ Board members. The Board is responsible for maintaining the overall policy and direction of the organization. The Board shall delegate responsibility of day-to-day operations to the Executive Director and appropriate committees. Board members shall receive no compensation (other than reasonable expenses) for their service on the Board. (*If you'd like to offer compensation such as reduced tuition or fees, state that here.*)

Section 2 – The Board shall meet at least ____ times per year at an agreed upon time and location. Board members shall not miss more than ____ meeting(s) per year.

Section 3 – All Board members shall serve for ____ year terms (staggered terms are optional) and can be eligible for re-election _____ times.

Section 4 – Any Director may be removed from office without assigning any cause by the vote of the Board at any meeting of the Board.

Section 5 – Any Director may resign at any time by giving notice to the organization.

Section 6 – In the event of a vacancy on the Board (including situations where the number of Board members has been deemed necessary to increase), the directors shall fill the vacancy.

Section 7 – A quorum must be attended by at least ____ percent of the Board members before business can be transacted or motions made or passed.

Article 5 – Officers

Section 1 – The officers of the organization shall be _____, _____, _____, _____. *(Position title such as Director, President, Secretary, Treasurer, not names)* The Board of Directors shall appoint each of these officers. The Board may also appoint other officers it deems necessary.

Section 2 – The Board of Directors shall appoint officers for a term established by the Board.

Section 3 – Any officer may be removed from office without assigning any cause by the vote of the Board at any meeting of the Board.

Section 4 – Officers of the Board will not be compensated via salary for their service as an officer of the Board.

Section 5 – Board Chair/President (choose any title you wish)

The Chair shall convene regularly scheduled Board meetings and shall preside or arrange for other Directors to preside at each meeting in the following order: Vice Chair, Secretary and Treasurer. The Board Chair appoints Committee Chairs.

Section 6 – Vice Chair

The Vice Chair will chair committees on special subjects as designated by the board. In addition, the Vice Chair will facilitate meetings in the absence of the Board Chair.

Section 7 – Secretary

The Secretary shall be responsible for keeping records of Board actions, including overseeing the taking of minutes at all board meetings, sending out meeting announcements, distributing copies of minutes and the agenda to each Board member, and assuring that corporate records are maintained.

Section 8 – Treasurer

The Treasurer shall make a report at each Board meeting. The treasurer shall assist in the preparation of the budget, help develop fund raising plans, and make financial information available to Board members and the public.

Article 6 – Committees

Section 1 – The Board may create committees as needed, such as fund raising, registration, and special event committees. The Board Chair shall appoint all committee chairs.

Section 2 – No committee shall have any power to: fill vacancies on the Board, adopt amend or repeal the bylaws, amend or repeal any resolution of the Board, or act on matters committed by the bylaws or resolution of the Board to another committee of the Board.

Article 7 - IRC 501(c)3 Tax Exemption Provisions

These are paragraphs that the IRS expects to see. They are required to be a part of your Articles of Incorporation, but many organizations repeat the provisions in their bylaws.

a. Upon the dissolution of _____, assets shall be distributed for one or more exempt purposes within the meaning of section 501(c)(3) of the Internal Revenue Code, or corresponding section of any future federal tax code, or shall be distributed to the federal government, or to a state or local government, for public purpose.

b. _____ is organized exclusively for charitable, religious, educational, and/or scientific purposes under section 501(c)(3) of the Internal Revenue Code. No part of the net earnings of _____ shall inure to the benefit of, or be distributable to its members, trustees, officers, or other private persons, except that the organization shall be authorized and empowered to pay reasonable compensation for services rendered and to make payments and distributions in furtherance of the purposes set forth in the purpose clause hereof.

c. No substantial part of the activities of _____ shall be the carrying on of propaganda, or otherwise attempting to influence legislation, and the organization shall not participate in, or intervene in (including the publishing or distribution of statements) any political campaign on behalf of any candidate for public office.

d. Notwithstanding any other provision of this document, the organization shall not carry on any other activities not permitted to be carried on (a) by an organization exempt from federal income tax under section 501(c)(3) of the Internal Revenue Code, or corresponding section of any future federal tax code, or (b) by an organization, contributions to which are deductible under section 170(c)(2) of the Internal Revenue Code, or corresponding section of any future federal tax code.

Article 8 – Amendments

Section 1 – These bylaws may be amended when deemed necessary by a _____ majority vote of the Board of Directors. Proposed amendments must be submitted to _____ *(Whom? Secretary, Board Chair)* and sent along with regular board meeting notices.

III. Sample Articles of Incorporation

Checklist

Articles of Incorporation need to pass several "tests" in order to be acceptable to both your state and the IRS. Make sure your Articles pass this test. Use it as a final checklist. If you fill it out as you create your Articles, it will make the 501(c)(3) tax exempt application process easier. The IRS application, Form 1023 asks for article number and paragraph number for several items.

Organization Name: _____

State of Incorporation: _____

Date of Incorporation: _____

Purpose clause: The organization is exclusively formed to accomplish one or more of the eight specified 501(c)(3) purposes—charitable, religious, educational, scientific, testing for public safety, literary, fostering national or international amateur sports competition, or preventing cruelty to children or animals. Article & Paragraph Number:_____

Use of assets: The assets are permanently dedicated and substantially all of the funds must be spent for (c)(3) purposes. Article & Paragraph Number:_____

Dissolution clause: If the organization dissolves or otherwise ceases to operate, its assets must be paid over to another (c)(3) organization. Article & Paragraph Number:_____

Electioneering: The organization is prohibited from participating or intervening in any political campaign on behalf of any candidate for public office. Article & Paragraph Number:_____

Lobbying activity: No substantial part of the activities of the organization will be directed to conducting propaganda or otherwise attempting to influence legislation. Article & Paragraph Number:_____

Private inurement: No part of the net earnings of the organization, except for payment of reasonable compensation for services rendered, can be devoted to the personal or private interest of the directors, officers, or other individuals. No payments will be made to individuals upon dissolution. Article & Paragraph Number:_____

The IRS is quite helpful in supplying a sample Articles of Incorporation in their publications. It is pretty straightforward and you know it will be accepted in your application for tax-exempt status.

ARTICLES OF ORGANIZATION FROM IRS PUB 557 TAX-EXEMPT STATUS FOR YOUR ORGANIZATION

Articles of Incorporation of the undersigned, a majority of whom are citizens of the United States, desiring to form a nonprofit Corporation under the nonprofit Corporation Law of _____ (your state), do hereby certify:

First: The name of the Corporation shall be _____.

Second: The place in this state where the principal office of the Corporation is to be located is the City of _____, _____County, State of _____.

Third: Said corporation is organized exclusively for charitable, religious, educational, and scientific purposes, including, for such purposes, the making of distributions to organizations that qualify as exempt organizations under section 501(c)(3) of the Internal Revenue Code, or the corresponding section of any future federal tax code.

Fourth: The names and addresses of the persons who are the initial trustees of the corporation are as follows:

Name   Address

Fifth: No part of the net earnings of the corporation shall inure to the benefit of, or be distributable to its members, trustees, officers, or other private persons, except that the corporation shall be authorized and empowered to pay reasonable compensation for services rendered and to make payments and distributions in furtherance of the purposes set forth in Article Third hereof. No substantial part of the activities of the corporation shall be the carrying on of propaganda, or otherwise attempting to influence legislation, and the corporation shall not participate in, or intervene in (including the publishing or distribution of statements) any political campaign on behalf of or in opposition to any candidate for public office. Notwithstanding any other provision of these articles, the corporation shall not carry on any other activities not permitted to be carried on (a) by a corporation exempt from federal income tax under section 501(c)(3) of the Internal Revenue Code, or the corresponding section of any future federal tax code, or (b) by a corporation, contributions to which are deductible under section 170(c)(2) of the Internal Revenue Code, or the corresponding section of any future federal tax code.

If reference to federal law in articles of incorporation imposes a limitation that is invalid in your state, you may wish to substitute the following for the last sentence of the preceding paragraph: "Notwithstanding any other provision of these articles, this corporation shall not, except to an insubstantial degree, engage in any activities or exercise any powers that are not in furtherance of the purposes of this corporation."

Sixth: Upon the dissolution of the corporation, assets shall be distributed for one or more exempt purposes within the meaning of section 501(c)(3) of the Internal Revenue Code, or the corresponding section of any future federal tax code, or shall be distributed to the federal government, or to a state or local government, for a public purpose. Any such assets not so disposed of shall be disposed of by a Court of Competent Jurisdiction of the county in which the principal office of the corporation is then located, exclusively for such purposes or to such organization or organizations, as said Court shall determine, which are organized and operated exclusively for such purposes.

In witness whereof, we have hereunto subscribed our names this _____day of _____20__ .

SAMPLE ARTICLE OF INCORPORATION FOR HOMESCHOOL ORGANIZATION

Here is another sample Articles of Incorporation that I have adapted for homeschool organizations. The numbering differs slightly from the IRS sample, but is still acceptable.

Articles of Incorporation Of _____

Articles of Incorporation of the undersigned, a majority of whom are citizens of the United States, desiring to form a Nonprofit Corporation under the Nonprofit Corporation Law of _____ (your state's name), do hereby certify:

ARTICLE I The name of the Corporation shall be _____.

ARTICLE II The place in this state where the principal office of the Corporation is to be located is the City of _____, _____County.

ARTICLE III Said corporation is organized exclusively for charitable, religious, educational, and scientific purposes, including, for such purposes, the making of distributions to organizations that qualify as exempt organizations under section 501(c)(3) of the Internal Revenue Code, or the corresponding section of any future federal tax code.

ARTICLE IV The names and addresses of the persons who are the initial trustees of the corporation are as follows:

    Name   Address

ARTICLE V The qualifications for members and manner of their admissions are to be regulated by the bylaws.

ARTICLE VI No part of the net earnings of the corporation shall inure to the benefit of, or be distributable to its members, trustees, officers, or other private persons, except that the corporation shall be authorized and empowered to pay reasonable compensation for services rendered and to make payments and distributions in furtherance of the purposes set forth in Article Third hereof.

ARTICLE VII No substantial part of the activities of the corporation shall be the carrying on of propaganda, or otherwise attempting to influence legislation, and the corporation shall not participate in, or intervene in (including the publishing or distribution of statements) any political campaign on behalf of or in opposition to any candidate for public office. Notwithstanding any other provision of these articles, the corporation shall not carry on any other activities not permitted to be carried on (a) by a corporation exempt from federal income tax under section 501(c)(3) of the Internal Revenue Code, or the corresponding section of any future federal tax code, or (b) by a corporation, contributions to which are deductible under section 170(c)(2) of the Internal Revenue Code, or the corresponding section of any future federal tax code.

ARTICLE VIII Upon the dissolution of the corporation, assets shall be distributed for one or more exempt purposes within the meaning of section 501(c)(3) of the Internal Revenue Code, or the corresponding section of any future federal tax code, or shall be distributed to the federal government, or to a state or local government, for a public purpose. Any such assets not so disposed of shall be disposed of by a Court of Competent Jurisdiction of the county in which the principal office of the corporation is then located, exclusively for such purposes or to such organization or organizations, as said Court shall determine, which are organized and operated exclusively for such purposes.

In witness whereof, we have hereunto subscribed our names this _____day of _____, 20____.

IV. Sample Conflict of Interest Policies

The IRS provides this sample Conflict of Interest policy in its Instructions for Form 1023. The IRS version had specific paragraphs for hospitals that I have omitted, since they do not apply to homeschool groups.

IRS Sample Conflict of Interest Policy

Article I Purpose

The purpose of the conflict of interest policy is to protect this tax-exempt organization's (Organization) interest when it is contemplating entering into a transaction or arrangement that might benefit the private interest of an officer or director of the Organization or might result in a possible excess benefit transaction. This policy is intended to supplement but not replace any applicable state and federal laws governing conflict of interest applicable to nonprofit and charitable organizations.

Article II Definitions

1. Interested Person

Any director, principal officer, or member of a committee with governing board delegated powers, who has a direct or indirect financial interest, as defined below, is an interested person.

2. Financial Interest

A person has a financial interest if the person has, directly or indirectly, through business, investment, or family:

a. An ownership or investment interest in any entity with which the Organization has a transaction or arrangement,

b. A compensation arrangement with the Organization or with any entity or individual with which the Organization has a transaction or arrangement, or

c. A potential ownership or investment interest in, or compensation arrangement with, any entity or individual with which the Organization is negotiating a transaction or arrangement.

Compensation includes direct and indirect remuneration as well as gifts or favors that are not insubstantial.

A financial interest is not necessarily a conflict of interest. Under Article III, Section 2, a person who has a financial interest may have a conflict of interest only if the appropriate governing board or committee decides that a conflict of interest exists.

Article III Procedures

1. Duty to Disclose

In connection with any actual or possible conflict of interest, an interested person must disclose the existence of the financial interest and be given the opportunity to disclose all material facts to the directors and members of committees with governing board delegated powers considering the proposed transaction or arrangement.

2. Determining Whether a Conflict of Interest Exists

After disclosure of the financial interest and all material facts, and after any discussion with the interested person, he/she shall leave the governing board or committee meeting while the determination of a conflict of interest is discussed and voted upon. The remaining board or committee members shall decide if a conflict of interest exists.

3. Procedures for Addressing the Conflict of Interest

a. An interested person may make a presentation at the governing board or committee meeting, but after the presentation, he/she shall leave the meeting during the discussion of, and the vote on, the transaction or arrangement involving the possible conflict of interest.

b. The chairperson of the governing board or committee shall, if appropriate, appoint a disinterested person or committee to investigate alternatives to the proposed transaction or arrangement.

c. After exercising due diligence, the governing board or committee shall determine whether the Organization can obtain with reasonable efforts a more advantageous transaction or arrangement from a person or entity that would not give rise to a conflict of interest.

d. If a more advantageous transaction or arrangement is not reasonably possible under circumstances not producing a conflict of interest, the governing board or committee shall determine by a majority vote of the disinterested directors whether the transaction or arrangement is in the Organization's best interest, for its own benefit, and whether it is fair and reasonable. In conformity with the above determination it shall make its decision as to whether to enter into the transaction or arrangement.

It goes on like this for six more articles. I think you get the picture. It is a very formal and thorough policy. I think it may be overkill for most homeschool organizations. Use it if you like. See http://www.irs.gov/instructions/i1023/ar03.html for the entire policy.

Nonprofit Financial Center Sample Conflict of Interest Policy

Here's a much shorter Conflict of Interest policy from the Nonprofit Financial Center (www.nonprofitrisk.org) that may work for your group. It has each board member disclose businesses they own and other organizations they serve.

No member of the [Name of Nonprofit] Board of Directors or Staff shall derive any personal profit or gain, directly or indirectly, by reason of his or her participation in the [Name of Nonprofit]. Each individual shall disclose to the [Name of Nonprofit] any personal interest which he or she may have in any matter pending before the organization and shall refrain from participation in any decision on such matter. Any member of the [Name of Nonprofit]'s Board of Directors or Staff shall refrain from obtaining any list of [Name of Nonprofit] clients for personal or private solicitation purposes at any time during the term of their affiliation.

In addition to my service for [Name of Nonprofit], at this time I am a Board member or an employee of the following organizations:

1.

2.

3.

4.

This is to certify that I, except with regard to carrying out my duties as an officer, director or staff member of the [Name of Nonprofit] or as described below, am not now nor at any time during the past year have been:

A participant, directly or indirectly, in any arrangement, agreement, investment, or other activity with any vendor, supplier, or other party; doing business with the [Name of Nonprofit] which has resulted or could result in person benefit to me.

A recipient, directly or indirectly, of any salary payments or loans or gifts of any kind or any free service or discounts or other fees from or on behalf of any person or organization engaged in any transaction with the [Name of Nonprofit].

Any exceptions to 1 or 2 above are stated below with a full description of the transactions and of the interest, whether direct or indirect, which I have (or have had during the past year) in the persons or organizations having transactions with the [Name of Nonprofit].

Signature: _____ Date _____

Printed name: _____

BOARD CAFÉ SAMPLE CONFLICT OF INTEREST POLICY

Here's a plain language policy from Board Cafe (www.compasspoint.org/bookstore) that states the ultimate purpose of a conflict of interest policy – to put the nonprofit's best interests before personal interest. I like its emphasis on using good judgment.

The standard of behavior at the _____ Nonprofit is that all staff, volunteers, and board members scrupulously avoid any conflict of interest between the interests of the Organization on one hand, and personal, professional, and business interests on the other. This includes avoiding actual conflicts of interest as well as perceptions of conflicts of interest.

I understand that the purposes of this policy are: to protect the integrity of the Organization's decision-making process, to enable our constituencies to have confidence in our integrity, and to protect the integrity and reputation of volunteers, staff and board members.

Upon or before election, hiring or appointment, I will make a full, written disclosure of interests, relationships, and holdings that could potentially result in a conflict of interest. This written disclosure will be kept on file and I will update it as appropriate.

In the course of meetings or activities, I will disclose any interests in a transaction or decision where I (including my business or other nonprofit affiliation), my family and/or my significant other, employer, or close associates will receive a benefit or gain. After disclosure, I understand that I will be asked to leave the room for the discussion and will not be permitted to vote on the question.

I understand that this policy is meant to be a supplement to good judgment, and I will respect its spirit as well as its wording.

Signed: _____ Date: _____

I hope that your organization can find and adopt a workable Conflict of Interest policy from the samples offered here. Feel free to modify any of the policies to best fit your organization.

About the Author

Carol L. Topp, CPA, is an accountant and a retired homeschooling mother. She earned her Bachelor of Science degree from Purdue University and worked as a Cost Analyst for the US Navy for ten years. In 2000, Carol passed the Certified Public Accountant (CPA) examination. Carol began homeschooling her two daughters since they started first grade. They are now homeschool high school graduates. She was very active in her local homeschool community teaching classes and speaking at support group meetings.

As an accountant, Carol has served on several not-for-profit boards. She has helped consulted with leaders from over 150 homeschool organizations and helped more than 50 organizations obtain 501(c) tax-exempt status. In addition, Carol prepares the annual Form 990 reporting with the Internal Revenue Service (IRS) for several homeschool and nonprofit groups. In 2006, Carol launched her website www.HomeschoolCPA.com to help homeschool organizations lead successful groups. It was voted a Top Accounting Blog in 2012.

She is the author of *Homeschool Co-ops: How to Start Them, Run Them and Not Burn Out, The IRS and Your Homeschool Organization, Money Management in a Homeschool Organization: A Guide for Treasurers* and the ebook *Paying Workers in a Homeschool Organization*.

Carol's publications include numerous articles, podcasts and webinars about operating a homeschool nonprofit. Her articles have appeared in The Old Schoolhouse, Home Education and Home School Enrichment magazines. In addition, Carol has enjoyed conducting workshops for homeschool leaders at conventions across the country.

As a professional accountant, Carol's affiliations include the Ohio Society of CPAs, the National Association of Tax Professionals, The Ohio Society of CPAs Speakers Bureau, and The Ohio Society's Financial Literacy Committee.

Carol lives in Cincinnati, Ohio with her husband where she enjoys reading, traveling, and helping homeschool leaders. Carol can be contacted through her website www.HomeschoolCPA .

Visit www.HomeschoolCPA.com .

Sign-up for a monthly newsletter, Homeschool Leader, that answers questions from homeschool leaders like you.

Carol Topp, CPA has authors other books for homeschool leaders.

Homeschool Co-ops: How to Start Them, Run Them and Not Burn Out

Money Management for Homeschool Organizations

Paying Workers in a Homeschool Organization (ebook only)

Questions and Answers for Homeschool Leaders (ebook only)

If this book has been helpful to you, please leave a positive review at Amazon.com **http://tinyurl.com/pfcqbuj**
Even just a short sentence would be appreciated! Thank you!

Index

Notes

[1] A History of the Tax Exempt Sector. http://www.irs.gov/pub/irs-soi/tehistory.pdf

[2] http://www.oecdobserver.org/news/fullstory.php/aid/2954/Charities_and_tax_abuse.html

[3] http://en.wikipedia.org/wiki/Boy_Scouts_of_America_v._Dale

[4] http://www.law.cornell.edu/uscode/html/uscode26/usc_sec_26_00000501----000-.html

[5] http://www.law.cornell.edu/uscode/html/uscode26/usc_sec_26_00000501----000-.html

[6] http://en.wikipedia.org/wiki/501(c)

[7] IRS webinar: "Starting Off Right: What New Non-501c (3) Organizations Need to Know." Feb 24, 2011, page 39

[8] http://www.irs.gov/pub/irs-tege/rr58-589.pdf; http://www.irs.gov/publications/p557/ch04.html#en_US_2010_publink1000200325 and http://www.irs.gov/irm/part7/irm_07-025-007.html

[9] http://www.irs.gov/charities/charitable/article/0,,id=123297,00.html

[10] 501(c)(3) organizations do not pay tax on the exempt function income. If they have income from sources unrelated to their exempt purpose, they may be subject to an unrelated business income tax (UBIT).

[11] http://charitylawyerblog.com/2011/04/26/nonprofit-law-jargon-buster-voting-members-vs-self-perpetuating-boards/

[12] http://www.urban.org/uploadedpdf/412386-Organizations-that-Lost-their-Tax-Exempt-Status.pdf

Made in the USA
San Bernardino, CA
12 March 2020

65575724R00073